RANDOM
HOUSE

LARGE
PRINT

Praise for
MISSION POSSIBLE

"Tim is the perfect author for a book that encourages readers to make their lives count. The principles he talks about reflect not only his passion but also the vision for his life that he actively pursues. When you take this journey through these pages with Tim, one thing is clear: you're going to discover purpose wherever you are and leave an impact wherever you go. If you want to do much more than just occupy space in this life, pick up this book and let Tim show you how."
—THOMAS RHETT AKINS, country music artist and 2021 ACM Awards Male Artist of the Year

"For years I've watched my friend Tim Tebow pursue various passions—each of them with all his heart, mind, and strength. No matter the challenges or opinions he faced, his faith in the greater purpose was unwavering. His perseverance remains the same today, and I believe **Mission Possible** will help you know why you, too, can embody that mindset in whatever passion you're pursuing."
—STEPHEN A. SMITH, sports journalist, radio host, and ESPN commentator

"No matter who you are or where you are from, God has a plan for your life. Understanding His plan can become quite challenging for those who aren't equipped with the right tools. **Mission Possible** will help you deal with what God has in store for you. Tim allows us to see that God's plan has purpose even though we may not see it clearly at times."

—LUKE BRYAN, country music artist and five-time ACM Awards Entertainer of the Year

"**Mission Possible** is timely and timeless. Each chapter is written with intentionality, emphasizing a sense of urgency to discover what it means to make your life count. It doesn't matter your background, title, zip code, or perceived limitations; Tim reminds you that God created us all to live each day with purpose. And in this book, Tim will show you how. When you turn the final page, get ready to be, as he calls it, 'a champion of higher purpose.'"

—STEVEN FURTICK, **New York Times** bestselling author and pastor of Elevation Church

MISSION POSSIBLE

MISSION POSSIBLE

Go Create a Life That Counts

Tim Tebow

with A. J. Gregory

RANDOM HOUSE
LARGE PRINT

Published in the United States of America by Random House Large Print in association with Waterbrook, an imprint of Random House, a division of Penguin Random House LLC.

Cover design: Mission Driven Studios
Cover photograph: © Adam Szarmack/Mission Driven Studios

The Library of Congress has established a Cataloging-in-Publication record for this title.

ISBN: 978-0-593-55938-3

www.penguinrandomhouse.com/large-print-format-books

FIRST LARGE PRINT EDITION

Printed in the United States of America

1st Printing

This Large Print edition published in accord with the standards of the N.A.V.H.

To Jesus, the only one through whom we can live mission possible, and to everyone who has ever given and will give whatever they have, a lot or a little, to make other people's lives better—you have truly made your lives count.

CONTENTS

Introduction   xi

1 Mission Proposal, Mission Purpose   3

2 God Possible, Purpose Possible   31

3 Right Where You Are   51

4 Mission-Possible Superpowers   77

5 Purpose in the Present   101

6 Purpose in the Resistance   129

7 Elevate Convictions over Emotions   153

8 Embrace the Grind   175

9 Purpose in the Waiting   201

10 Your Life Counts   229

A Special Invitation   249

Notes   251

INTRODUCTION

BEFORE MARRYING DEMI, ONE OF the questions I was most often asked was, "Who are you dating?" Lately, though, I've heard a lot of questions like, "What is God's will for my life?" Or sometimes it's phrased differently, like, "How can I find my calling?" or "What is my purpose?"

I've often wondered what those words even mean when we use them like that. I know what Merriam and Webster have decided, but how often have you heard those words dropped as a cliché in conversation? What do they really mean? When people ask these kinds of questions, what kind of answer are they looking for? Are they hoping for a general answer: "to love and serve God and others"? Or a specific answer about career: "You should become a doctor"? Or just an answer about making a difference: "helping the poor or those who are underprivileged"? Or are they looking for something more glamorous, like becoming a bestselling author or winning an Emmy?

Am I asking too many questions when you're hoping to find some answers?

All these questions about purpose remind me of a comedic conversation in **The Hobbit.** After finishing his breakfast, Bilbo Baggins is standing by his front door, when none other than Gandalf comes waltzing by. Bilbo nods at the old wizard and says, "Good morning." It's a typical early-day greeting that requires nothing more than a nod and a smile. But Gandalf is too deep for that.

He says to Bilbo, "Do you wish me a good morning, or mean that it is a good morning whether I want it or not; or that you feel good this morning; or that it is a morning to be good on?"[1]

I suppose we each have a little Gandalf in us. We can get hung up on questions or confused by semantics instead of taking action, even just one little step.

Scripture gives us one shared and big-picture purpose: to glorify God. As believers, we honor and serve Him with our lives, our natural gifts, our resources, our bodies, our worship, and our decisions. The list is vast, but the goal is clear. In His last instructions to His disciples, Jesus commanded them to "go, therefore, and make disciples of all the nations, baptizing them in the name of the Father and the Son and the Holy Spirit, teaching them to follow all that I commanded you; and behold, I am with you always, to the end of the age" (Matthew 28:19–20).

I like to think of this command as marching orders for the church.

> **When you live mission possible, you live a life that counts because of what God has done and is doing through you.**

Now, this scriptural charge doesn't mean that you have to become a missionary or plant yourself on the other side of the world. Nor does it mean that you have to sing worship songs during every waking hour (though if you feel a tug on your heart to do that, go for it!). But it does mean that your big-picture purpose is to bring glory to God wherever you are.

After, and only after, you latch on to that God-given, big-picture purpose, there's a way to identify what your personal purpose might be.

Within that greater purpose of glorifying God, you find your purpose in what you do every day. Simply put, purpose is about being mission driven in your ordinary life.

Living a mission-possible life means executing the good works that God has already prepared for you to do. This is what Paul was talking about when he wrote, "We are His workmanship, created in Christ Jesus for good works, which God prepared beforehand so that we would walk in them" (Ephesians 2:10).

You can live a mission-possible life because of what Jesus did for you on the cross more than two thousand years ago. This kind of life is possible only because of the sacrifice He made and the power given to Him to trample over death. When you live mission possible, you live a life that counts because of what God has done and is doing through you.

We are each on a mission to make a difference: a mission to help the hurting; a mission to reach the last, the lost, and the least. It looks different for everyone. It might take you into the darkness on a rescue mission to those who are being human trafficked. It might keep you home in your own neighborhood, breathing life and spirit into your children or your neighbors. When you are mission driven, you use your ability and God's empowerment to help, serve, guide, teach, pray, and lead others in innumerable ways as unique as each person's DNA. Doing that is mission possible because of who equips and walks with you in the process.

Here's a surprise for you: mission is not really as mysterious as we make it out to be. And it's more available to you than you ever imagined.

Have you ever been going about your daily life, when suddenly, out of nowhere, your heart is drawn to a need or toward a person who might be struggling? Maybe an image of a cousin who is battling an opioid addiction pops into your head, or you think of the single mom in the neighborhood struggling to balance remote learning with her work schedule, or you remember a social media post about a certain organization that is helping orphans in another country. The world is flooded with hurting people and messed-up situations. And while we cannot fix every problem, God can. And through our willingness, we can partner with Him and bring some light to a world that is shadowed with darkness.

So if God opens your eyes to a situation and pricks your heart to get involved, take a step in that direction. And another step after that. Left. Right. Repeat.

I wasn't always driven to help people with special needs. I felt a pull in that direction when I met a little boy in the Philippines with his feet on backward. It was then that my passion grew to help people. That's why, in 2010, I was so excited to create the Tim Tebow Foundation (TTF) with a mission "to bring faith, hope, and love to those needing a brighter day in their darkest hour of need."[2] Looking back, I can connect the dots and recognize my parents' strong influence that shaped me and my other siblings to live a mission-possible life.

God has designed you so that you don't have to bumble your way through life. I believe He wants you to find your purpose. There are times we're already walking in our purpose and we might not even know it! Sometimes God makes it clear, and sometimes it might not feel that way. That's why it's called living by faith, not by sight.

By using what He has already given us right where we are, we can make a positive difference in this world. This is my mission, and it's yours too. Being intentional about living mission possible will:

- guide your priorities
- align your responsibilities and decisions with what's right
- fuel your drive and passion
- set your sights on eternity

Living with a mission-impossible mindset is dangerous. Deadly, even. We know things like smoking and living off junk food will never increase our vitality or longevity. But did you know that if you lack meaning in your life, you risk an early death? According to **Psychosomatic Medicine: Journal of Biobehavioral Medicine,** researchers reviewed the correlation between purpose in life and mortality by analyzing participants between ages fifty-one and sixty-one. It was found that "people without a strong life purpose were more than twice as likely to die between the study years of 2006 and 2010, compared with those who had one."[3] I'm not trying to freak you out with this truth or add to your overextended goal list. Not at all. In fact, I want this book to refresh you.

> **Living with a mission-impossible mindset is dangerous.**

If your spirit has faded over the last few months or years, I want to ignite a new spark in your life. I want to show you that wherever you are and in whatever you do, not only can you find meaning but you can accomplish a mission that you have already been called to and equipped for. It's never too early or too late to start thinking about living a mission-possible life.

One of the greatest lies the devil ever told was that our lives don't matter: **You'll never be good enough. You have too much baggage. What about that skeleton in your closet?** Have you ever heard those things whispered in your ear at night when all your friends have gone home and the screens are powered down?

It's hard to live mission possible when we don't fully believe that we are made in God's image, hand-chosen by Him and fully equipped to carry out works of eternal significance. It's actually impossible. You will never come to believe that your life counts if you think you are here by accident or you're stuck in a space where you're just going through the motions.

Lean in a bit. If you have made the decision to trust in Jesus, you're not just an average person who got slightly better. You were someone who was dead to sin who is now alive in Christ. Take a moment and read that again: you were dead, and now you are alive. Wow!

Through His death and resurrection, Jesus has brought each of us from:

old to new,
dead to alive,
sin to righteousness,
slave to son or daughter,
bondage to freedom,
darkness to light,
lost to found.

I hope that fires you up as much as it does me. When I reflect on this drastic trade, it makes me feel so alive and empowered that I can't help but feel driven to influence others. I want the same for you.

When you believe that you are valuable and worthy because of who lives inside you, everything changes. You find meaning. You live with purpose. Significance exists within each day. And when you soak in the truth that you were created in the image of God, by love, in love, and for love, you begin to see the world differently. You see people in a new light. Your eyes open to hurt, and your heart bleeds for the hurting. Your priorities shift and you begin to understand that it doesn't matter how successful you are—that significance matters more. And significance is found when you align your soul with what matters to God and move forward each day.

Jesus was made flesh to walk this earth not so He could perform mind-blowing tricks on people. Yes, healing and other mighty miracles were part of the plan. Yet, ultimately, Jesus was on a rescue mission to save our souls. Christianity isn't about being perfect. It's not even about being good or giving one's money away. Christianity is about having a relationship with the God of this universe, through His Son, Jesus. And once we are in that relationship, we want to help people—not because we have to, but because we have the privilege of serving the Creator of this universe since we are intimately connected with Him. That's why we're here. That's why we fight for people around the world and honor God when we do it.

Significance exists within each day.

You can feel bad for orphans who live in shacks without running water halfway around the world. But if it doesn't move you enough to do something about it, you might be missing what God has called each of us to do. Feed the hungry. Clothe the naked. Care for the widows. Defend the cause of the poor. Speak up for those who can't speak up for themselves. Help the weak. Rescue those who are oppressed. Be generous. Show mercy. These are all missions! And I didn't make them up. They are all found in Scripture.

I want to encourage you to be part of a rescue mission for people. Don't live with the goal of just getting by. Live with a greater significance than achievements, accolades, or an impressive bio. With purpose, your life overflows with meaning. You are alive because you are connected to the source of all creation. God has a plan for you to love and care for people. You honor Him through that mission.

Tom Cruise gets major props for doing most of his stunts in the eight **Mission: Impossible** films. He plays Ethan Hunt, an agent of the Impossible Missions Force who, with his spy team, will save the world. As Ethan Hunt, Cruise engages in stunts that require serious training, defy gravity, and pose the risk of death.

In **Ghost Protocol,** Cruise scales and hangs off the tallest building in the world: a Dubai skyscraper that stands 2,722 feet tall. Oh, and he's using only a pair of climbing gloves to do it. We find Cruise fiddling with an underwater security system in **Rogue Nation** and having to hold his breath for six minutes. The average person can hold his or her breath for one or two minutes. That same movie features Cruise dangling off an Airbus A400M while it takes off, reaches an altitude of about 5,000 feet at 184 miles per hour, and then lands.[4] Cruise was wearing a harness, but still. Then there's the opening scene in **Mission: Impossible 2**—the one where Cruise hangs from a cliff, holding on to the ledge with his bare hands. He was fitted with a safety harness but refused a safety net.

My favorite scene is found in the first **Mission: Impossible.** It's arguably the most memorable in the franchise. Cruise executes a high-wire dive in the CIA building to hack a computer in a pressure-sensitive and secured vault. Most of the stunt is performed by Cruise. It's his core and balance at work while being suspended in one position, perfectly still.

These stunts seem impossible for most of us. I don't know many people who would hang off the edge of a cliff by their hands or who would even want to try, for that matter. **It's dangerous. It's risky. What if a cable snaps or a harness is clipped the wrong way? What if it gets windy? It's physically impossible.** I imagine that's what most of us would say if asked to pilot a helicopter chase or climb a tower almost twice as high as the Empire State Building.

We have similar excuses that keep us from being mission driven. **It's too hard. I don't know where to start. I'm sick/tired/broke/busy.** The good news is that your mission is always possible when God is involved. Jesus may not have been pushed out of a plane at twenty-five thousand feet, but He did something more daring that's not only jaw dropping but life changing: He defeated death. And if you are serving a God who has rattled the doors of hell and trampled over death, you can fulfill whatever He has called you to do.

In this book, I'm going to show you how to become a champion of higher purpose, as mandated in Scripture. You'll learn how to share the hope of Jesus through service and how to move the mission forward each day, even when it feels dull or frightening or unfamiliar. I'll show you how to develop a mission life statement that is biblical and takes into account God-given talents, skills, and opportunities. I'll teach you the mindset and commitment required to live a mission-possible life each day. I'll remind you how important it is to prioritize convictions over feelings, and I'll walk with you as you learn how to do it.

And my hope is that when you're done reading this, you begin to live your life with a deeper sense of purpose, meaning, and significance than ever before and make your life count. As your relationship with God deepens, you will become more aware of His promptings, whether the whispers in your heart or the principles that come alive in His Word. You will understand that you are God's masterpiece, created to do good things in your own unique way on your own unique journey. You will become more intentional about living a mission-possible life, using your gifts, resources, and where you are to further the greater purpose of loving and serving God and others and make a lasting mark on this life, knowing you can because He did.

Our time on earth is limited. I want to do things that matter. I'm so honored to be able to play sports, write books, and motivate others. But I'm most passionate about bringing faith, hope, and love to those needing light in their darkest hour through the work we do at my foundation. I base my priorities on what's in my heart, and I try to live out of that passion, trusting that when I fall short or don't have a map for what's next, God has it all under control.

In one of the scenes of the original **Mission: Impossible,** Ethan Hunt sits on a train with his three future accomplices. With breezy confidence, he lays out their mission, a laundry list of one insurmountable task after another. The expressions of his cohorts are priceless. Shock and disbelief flood their faces. When Hunt finishes outlining his elaborate plan, one of them blurts out, "Are you sure we can do this?"[5]

Without missing a beat, Hunt replies, "We're going to do it." Cue **Mission: Impossible** theme song.

We serve a God who is much bigger than an impressive character in a fictional movie. We serve the God of this universe, who holds life itself in His hands. He is in this with you. He is beside you. He is rooting for you, and He is fighting for you.

Today you can begin to live your life on a trajectory that sets you up to accomplish feats of eternal purpose. Remember, with Him, all things are possible. Maybe God is whispering in your ear right now, **We're going to do it.**

Let's take that first step, together.

MISSION POSSIBLE

1

MISSION PROPOSAL, MISSION PURPOSE

I've always believed the mission is greater than the man.
—RICK PERRY

THE SIERRA MADRE HAS ONE OF THE largest rain forests in the Philippines. Situated on the island of Luzon, this rugged jungle is home to a surviving hunter-gatherer group called the Agta. Several years ago, a group of anthropologists set out to study this Indigenous group of people. The researchers were curious to learn more about how the Agta valued the members of their tribe based on their individual contributions. You'd think the ones who had skills like hunting, gathering, and fishing would top the list, but that wasn't the case. You know who came out on top? Storytellers.[1] The Agta revered the tribe members who spun tales more than those who literally brought home the bacon, the snacks, and the drinks.

While it's clear they hold it in high esteem, the Agta aren't the only ones who appreciate the art of storytelling.

Stories matter. They're important. They flavor what might otherwise be a boring lecture. They keep us entertained while we binge-watch shows on Netflix. Stories can engage and inspire and have an effect on a single life or go on to change thousands.

Who doesn't love a good story?

And who doesn't love telling one?

When I began to scheme about how to propose to my then girlfriend, Demi, I knew it had to be a great story. I wanted to offer my future bride an experience that would spark memories of joy throughout her lifetime. I wanted her to sigh in bliss and get butterflies in her stomach whenever she'd recall what I hoped would be one of the best days of her life. I wanted her to be reminded of how much she is loved.

Okay, fine, and maybe, just maybe, there was a smidgen of ego in my motivation. I wanted to be the awesome fiancé who crushed this monumental task. What can I say? I'm a competitive guy, even with myself.

There are a few elements necessary to create an experience that will live on as a great story, particularly an engagement story. I knew that to make it meaningful to Demi, this moment had to include special people, a beautiful location, and the element of surprise. The goal was to have a mission possible, mission proposal for the girl of my dreams.

The ring had to come from Africa, my bride's homeland. Over the past few months of dating, Demi had dropped a few hints about the styles of rings she liked. They were clues, but I knew the finished product was up to me. After I met with several different jewelers, one in particular had some great recommendations. Over the next few months, Tom Hoyt and I had many conversations about finding the perfect ring, but when he started talking about an "internally flawless diamond," which is exactly what it sounds like, well, he had my attention. To make matters even more interesting, the responsibly sourced ring had a story of its own, recorded in a beautifully designed book.

Giving gifts is my love language. Having found a woman who, to me, was the epitome of flawless beauty in so many ways, I knew this was the ring for her. The diamond included an artfully crafted book that described its journey. Discovered in 2014, the gem qualified as "exceptional" because it was so rare and valuable. It was kept separate from other diamonds from the moment it was found. A company in New York cut and polished the diamond, and it took five craftsmen to bring this masterpiece to its final form.

The diamond then traveled from New York to Belgium and underwent a twenty-seven-step evaluation process by renowned gemologists and diamond graders. Together they confirmed the diamond was beautiful enough and met the clarity, cut, and color requirements to carry the Forevermark promise. Many diamonds get rejected during this process. Demi's, however, a diamond of exceptional beauty, passed with flying colors. I love that it had a unique story, like Demi, and they both came from Africa, and I couldn't wait for those two stories to come together.

I had found something beautiful to give to the love of my life. But creating an element of surprise proved a bit more difficult. Unbeknownst to Demi, I had arranged for my family, both sets of her parents, and her best friends to be present the moment I popped the question. It's hard enough to coordinate the schedules of two or three buddies to watch college football at my house, let alone twenty-plus loved ones from around the world. It proved a challenge, but with a lot of help from others, it happened. Special people? Check.

The big moment would come on January 9, after a belated and (wink, wink) faux Christmas celebration with my family in Florida. Over the actual holidays, I was helping report on the national championship between Clemson and Alabama for **SEC Nation** and ESPN. Demi and I flew from South Africa, where we had spent the holidays, to the States. At the ESPN party before the big game on January 7, Demi and I met the president of Clemson, Jim

Clements, and his wife, Beth. They are some of the sweetest people you'll ever meet. They have four children—including a daughter named Grace, who has special needs—and host a Night to Shine event in their community. The four of us became fast friends. Fast-forward to the pregame show. Right after filming for **SEC Nation,** I looked around and noticed Demi was nowhere to be found. I sent her a text saying I had to be down on the field for the first part of the game but that we could meet up after. Her reply was shocking: "That's fine! I'm hanging out with Jim and Beth in their box!"

What?? As a good southern boy would say, "Bless her heart." I mean, Jim and Beth are absolutely wonderful people, but Demi doesn't understand the finer nuances of American football allegiances! While I don't necessarily root for Alabama, I do work for **SEC Nation.** By the way, the whole debacle says a lot about my wife. She may not have realized the difference between the Atlantic Coast Conference (ACC) and the Southeastern Conference (SEC), but even if she had, I know that Demi always looks past what other people might see and appreciates people just for who they are. It's one of many reasons I fell in love with her. Clemson won that night. I guess she picked the right winner that day—and ultimately the right husband. When I got up to the box later on, I was shocked. You might say Demi was drinking the Clemson Kool-Aid. Her neck was adorned with an orange scarf, and she was holding orange pom-poms. I'm surprised she didn't have a claw painted on her cheek. Jim and Beth sure do know how to sell their team!

Demi and I arrived in Jacksonville, Florida, my hometown, on January 8. We spent the day celebrating "kid Christmas" first. All the nieces and nephews gathered together at my house and unwrapped their gifts, and then it was time for the adults to unwrap their gifts, one person at a time, one gift at a time. After each gift, we took time to talk about it. You can imagine how long the process took.

In order to create a proposal that was unexpected, I did something that you might think is borderline unfair. As we opened presents with my family that morning, I gave Demi a small velvet box. I knew what she really was hoping to find in that box, even though she'd never say it out loud. When the box clicked open, Demi's eyes widened and she beheld . . . not an engagement ring. She did her best to hide her disappointment and tried to be gracious and effusive about her present. My gift was strategic—a slight misdirection. I figured getting her a non-engagement ring would throw her off the scent if she had any expectations of getting a real one.

Once we finished opening gifts, it was time for Mission Proposal, which would happen in the backyard of my parents' farmhouse. The plan was for everyone to meet for dinner at my parents' house nearby. Some of the women were suggesting to Demi that she dress up since Christmas dinner at the Tebows' was a formal thing (not entirely true, by the way—more like jeans and T-shirts or pajamas). Before we left, and while most of the family had already arrived at Mom and Dad's, I had something else planned to further divert Demi from an engagement trail. A friend who worked at a local car dealership had dropped off a decoy truck that Demi thought she and I were going to drive over to my parents' to give my father as his last gift (sorry, Dad!). The day was ripe with sweet surprises but none for my soon-to-be fiancée. I was positive Demi had zero expectations of getting engaged that day.

Funny, on the drive over to my parents' place, one of our favorite songs just happened to come on. It was "The Wedding Song" by Demi's favorite South African artist, Matthew Mole—the very same musician I had flown in that day and had arranged to play live for her right after I'd ask her to marry me. The mood was perfectly set.

So much was happening around me that was intentional and planned according to a particular sequence of events. Friends and family who were helping with the scheduling aspect were discreetly checking their phones to make sure people were wherever they were supposed to be, particularly Demi's family and friends who were flying in from South Africa. A proposal was at stake! If one thing or one person fell out of order, the entire proposal would be ruined. The engagement and post-engagement pictures had to be taken during the last hour before sunset so the lighting could hit just right with the backyard scenery. Photographers had camouflaged themselves behind trees and bushes. Microphones had been planted inconspicuously so our loved ones back at the house could be part of the moment and be ready to join us on cue.

Finally, it was time. We pulled into the farm but didn't go inside the packed house. Instead, I asked Demi to follow me to the back of the house, where the pond was. I told her I had something to show her. The sun hung low on the horizon, radiating soft light around the backyard of my childhood home, where my parents still live. Crickets chirped in the background, and a slight breeze beckoned the trees to whisper in rhythm. Beautiful location? Check.

So many fond memories flooded my mind as the pond came into view. Demi knew the pond was special to me. It was where our family buried Otis, the dog I grew up with. And it would be where, ten months later, I would bury Bronco, my next dog. By that pond, I had prayed about where to go to college. And now another event was emerging that would change the course of both of our lives. Demi and I walked to a wooden archway adorned with white flowers canopied over a bench under which I had carved the following to mark the span of our dating relationship:

Timmy & Demi
4/28/2018–1/9/2019
Forever . . . My Sweets

I spoke from my heart. I can't tell you everything that was said, because that's just between me and her, but here are the lines that mean the most and I'll remember always: "Demi, I love you so much. I wanted to bring you here, to where I grew up, to a place that I love so much, so I could be with the person I love the most. When I first saw you, you gave me so much hope. When I first heard your voice, you gave me so much belief. When I first met you, I knew I wanted to spend the rest of my life fighting for you, fighting for us." I slipped down to the ground on one knee. "Will you marry me?"

She said yes.

After shedding a few tears and sharing some laughs, we held each other close as "The Wedding Song" played. It was a cue for the next scene in the story. As tears drenched Demi's eyes, a figure began to emerge from a stack of hay bales. It was Matthew Mole himself, strumming his guitar and serenading us live. Demi's face froze in shock. There he was, her favorite artist, playing for her right there in Jacksonville, Florida.

He was also the second cue. Demi and I swayed in rhythm to the melody as I gently rotated our bodies so the back deck of the house was out of her view. "I wish your family could be here right now," I whispered.

Demi nodded. "Me too," she said, sadness in her eyes. We danced while the sun continued its descent under the horizon. After a minute or two, I turned her around and she burst into tears. Her parents and their spouses were walking toward us with arms outstretched and not a dry eye. Third cue. During the tearful reunion, three of Demi's closest friends left the house and joined the tear fest. Fourth cue. Finally, my parents and sisters and brothers made their way toward the wooden archway. As loved ones followed their cues, photographers leaped from behind their secret places and snapped forever memories of the happy occasion. Demi was visibly overwhelmed. She looked radiant, positively happy. And just looking at her shine in that moment was worth every minute of planning and secrecy. The engagement proposal unfolded on schedule and exactly as planned.

I'll never forget what Demi told my dad when the night came to a close. "Mr. Tebow, I'm sorry you didn't get a new truck, but you're getting a new daughter!"

Mission accomplished.

Step into the Fight

When I look back on the effort, thought, and time I invested in creating a story Demi would be excited to retell a thousand times in the future, I remember my own sense of urgency and intentionality. While the grand gesture—the proposal—mattered, of course, the little gestures along the way were just as important. Every detail had to be ironed out. In the months before I asked Demi to marry me, I had spent time each day doing a task, however small, to ultimately accomplish the mission.

Now, while I don't approach every day with this much intention and focus and detail, there's something to be said about how mission driven I was in proposing to Demi. Focus serves us well. I want it to be infused into the way I live my entire life—including how I love Demi, serve and inspire others, pursue my dreams, and honor God. I want my actions to be fueled by passion, by an insatiable drive to live out the mission I believe God has called me to. It's not to be a football player or baseball player or author or commentator, even though I love doing all of those things and strive to do them well. But I want my life to be so much more than that. I want to live a mission-possible life. I always want to strive to bring faith, hope, and love to those needing a brighter day in their darkest hour of need. That's the mission statement of our foundation, and it's also my personal mission statement.

When we choose to trust God with our lives, we have a sense of a higher calling. We recognize that significance matters more than success. We are motivated not by what others think about us but by how God sees us. We make a difference not by what we wear or what we own but by living out each day in a way that brings glory to Him.

We are meant to do so much more than occupy space. We are called to teach, care, love, help, pitch in, bear the burdens of others, and fight for those who can't fight for themselves.

From as early as I can remember, my dad worked so hard to instill in my siblings and me a mission-driven mindset. Dad was always reminding us kids to make our lives count. Achievements are good things, he'd tell us, but they aren't our priority. He taught us the importance of loving what God loves and loving who God loves, which is (sneak peek!) humanity. This is a big part of each of our missions.

> **When we live mission-possible lives, we create a cycle of good, of service, of compassion, and of action that inspires others to continue.**

I'll never forget the day in 2013 when my dad called me from overseas and told me he had just rescued four young girls from traffickers. He was preaching at an underground conference in a remote country where Christians are persecuted. When the conference was over, he heard that there were four girls about to be sold. He took out all the money he had in his wallet, $1,250, and with that cash, he purchased the freedom of those girls.

I knew that day my life was going to change, because I entered a new fight. I said, "Dad, I don't know exactly what we're going to do, but we're going to do something." Our foundation built the first safe home to take care of those four girls. And then the next four. And the next four. And we're still going.

The day my dad purchased the freedom of those four girls was pivotal. It opened my eyes. I believe that once your eyes are open to something like that, you can never unsee what you've seen. Dad made a split-second decision to step into the fight, and immediately our foundation stepped in with him. We weren't prepared at first. We weren't totally sure of what we were doing and didn't have all the answers to our questions, but that mission-driven moment, when Dad stood up and chose to advocate for girls he didn't know and had never even met, was the beginning of a ripple effect still in motion today. This is what happens when we live mission-possible lives: we create a cycle of good, of service, of compassion, and of action that inspires others to continue.

A mission-possible life has less to do with us and more to do with others. Mission living means being motivated by something other than yourself. It's scary. It's also pretty exciting. It can be unpredictable (but in a good way). It will also require submitting your preferences to God, and sometimes that doesn't feel very good or doesn't make you look as favorable as you'd like. That is where trusting God becomes crucial. If you've made the decision to trust

Him, He gives you the mission and makes it possible. Trust that He's got better plans for your life than you do.

Purpose over Preference

A man named Jonah learned that the hard way. In the Old Testament, Jonah was a prophet from the nation of Israel. Today he'd be called a foreign missionary. One day, God gave this prophet a mission:

> Arise, go to Nineveh, the great city, and cry out against it, because their wickedness has come up before Me. (Jonah 1:2)

The inhabitants of the city of Nineveh, the capital of the ancient empire of Assyria, needed a come-to-Jesus awakening. This nation had long been a threat to the Israelites, and they weren't living right. God had given Jonah a simple task: preach.

Talk about a clear mission. There wasn't much up for debate. Now, this mandate wasn't unfamiliar to Jonah. The man wasn't your average Israelite. God had given him assignments before that Jonah had accomplished without putting up a fuss. But this time it was different. God's mission for Jonah was to preach to the Ninevites, but apparently doing so didn't align with the prophet's preferences. Jonah hated the Ninevites. They were bullies, cruel and mean, and in Jonah's eyes, they deserved to be destroyed, not given a chance to repent. God said, "Preach," but Jonah's decision was to run.

Recognizing the stark contrast between God's mission and his preferences, Jonah ran to a local port, bought a ticket, and set sail with other passengers for the city of Tarshish. I'm not quite sure if God rolled His eyes at that point, but I do know that He sent a powerful storm to get the prophet's attention. The raging wind and the pounding rain whipped the ship without mercy, threatening to break the vessel apart.

The sailors on board threw their cargo into the sea to lighten the load and prayed to their false gods for help. And Jonah? Well, he was curled up in bed, fast asleep in his onesie.

The sailors sensed that Jonah was somehow connected to the turbulent weather. They woke him up and interrogated him like a team of skilled FBI agents. **Who are you? Where are you from? What are you doing here? Whom do you serve?** Realizing the storm wasn't leaving anytime soon, Jonah fessed up and admitted the storm was probably his fault. Then he suggested they toss him overboard. Some of them must have thought that wasn't the worst idea they'd heard, but they hesitated at first. Eventually, they relented to Jonah's wish. And wouldn't you know it, by the time his shivering body hit the water, in an instant, there were clear blue skies.

I don't know how good of a swimmer Jonah was,

but he must have been freaking out while treading in waters so deep he couldn't see the bottom. As Jonah gasped for breath, a great fish shimmied close enough to swallow him whole. The prophet stayed in the creature's belly for three whole days. Before Jonah checked out of his aquatic Airbnb, he cried out to God and repented. Then God nudged the fish again and it vomited out Jonah. I know, gross.

Before Jonah had time to take a warm shower, God repeated his mission to him: "Arise, go to Nineveh, the great city, and proclaim to it the proclamation which I am going to tell you" (3:2). This time Jonah wised up. It took him three days to preach to the entire city. It was one of the most successful revivals in the Bible. Even the king repented. And instead of destroying the city because of its evil ways, God poured out compassion, love, and forgiveness. You'd think Jonah would be thrilled. I mean, it was like the best kind of Billy Graham crusade. Instead, the prophet's response was an enigma: "Please LORD, was this not what I said when I was still in my own country? Therefore in anticipation of this I fled to Tarshish, since I knew that You are a gracious and compassionate God, slow to anger and abundant in mercy, and One who relents of disaster. So now, LORD, please take my life from me, for death is better to me than life" (4:2–3). So dramatic.

What Jonah was really saying was that in overwhelming the Ninevites with kindness and mercy, God was at the same time destroying his career as a prophet. See, Jonah had already prophesied that God was going to demolish the city, and because God changed His mind, Jonah was going to look bad. The prophet was more concerned about what his fellow Israelites would think of him than about God fulfilling His greatest mission on earth: saving humankind.

You may not win a popularity contest by being mission driven, but you'll certainly gain the favor of your Father in heaven.

Before we roast Jonah for his narcissism, let's take a look inward. Have you ever been afraid to make a difference for God because it would make you look a certain way? Like weird according to the standard of this world? Have you ever sacrificed something He wanted you to do because it would make you uncomfortable or call into question how others perceived you? I think deep down many of us can relate to Jonah. You may not win a popularity contest by being mission driven, but you'll certainly gain the favor of your Father in heaven. And isn't that what counts?

I admire my dad's boldness, but it wasn't always that way for me. I remember going out to eat as a family, which wasn't often. We'd always pray before meals, even in public. For most, this means huddling up, bowing your head, and whispering a short and simple pre-dinner prayer. Dad would blast his prayers so loud that the patrons three tables over would hear, "because you alone, O Lord, walk on the wings of the wind" (see Psalm 104:3). I hate to say this, but there were times I'd slink low in my seat and cringe. Dad was never ashamed of making his faith known, because Jesus was always the most important thing to him. He didn't care if it made him look weird or the odd one out. I grew to admire and respect that about him and would get irritated at the people who would make fun of him for it (and there were many). If we want to make our lives count, we have to be a little different, to do things differently. Why would we want to be like everyone else?

The significance your life creates carries more value than what others think about you. Whenever you are forced to make a decision between purpose and preference, choose purpose. It'll win every time.

It's Time to Make a Statement

I mentioned in the introduction that living a mission-possible life requires executing the good works that God has already prepared for you to do.

Let's make this really practical. What does that mean in everyday life? A good start for living mission possible is to come up with a mission statement.

Before you begin, know that the purpose of having a mission statement is not just to have a mission statement; it's about discerning what God has placed in your heart. A mission statement will serve a purpose when it's put into action.

Grab a journal or open an app and start jotting down your thoughts in response to the following questions:

- What do you want your life to stand for?
- What are you uniquely put on this earth to achieve?
- What kind of legacy do you want to leave behind?
- What gifts, talents, skills, resources, and opportunities has God given you to use to serve Him and others?
- What's important to you?
- What problems do you see that you can contribute to solving?

Start writing your unique answers to these questions. Take your time. Don't worry about spelling or grammar or sounding eloquent or smart. When you're done, you can continue to narrow your focus until you come up with something aligned with your life and who God created you to be. It might be helpful to revisit the statement from time to time as you read this book. Think of it as a work in progress, one that you'll shape and grow as you learn more about what God's mission for your life might look like.

Here are some helpful tips as you begin to craft this statement:

- Focus on what you want, not what you don't want.
- Stay positive and self-affirming.
- Keep it short, simple, and concise—preferably a sentence or two at most.
- It doesn't necessarily have to be a complete sentence.
- Make it sound like you. Don't craft a statement that you think would make your mentor or life coach happy. Be you.

I love the mission statement of Steve Biondo, the president of our foundation: "Wake up. Serve. Repeat." It's short, sweet, and effective. Here are a few more examples from corporations that might be helpful as you excavate your thoughts:

- **JetBlue:** To inspire humanity—both in the air and on the ground.
- **LinkedIn:** To connect the world's professionals to make them more productive and successful.
- **Whole Foods:** Our deepest purpose as an organization is helping support the

health, well-being, and healing of both people—customers, Team Members, and business organizations in general—and the planet.

Articulating your mission in this way will help you live a more focused and prioritized life. It will also remind you of what matters most.

Live Like You're Running Out of Time

A few years ago, I was covering the Heisman ceremony for ESPN in New York City, where Demi, my fiancée at the time, lived. As crammed as our schedules were, I knew it'd be a real miss if I didn't plan something fun for us to do. At the last minute, I got tickets to see the Broadway show **Hamilton.** Lin-Manuel Miranda wrote this unique retelling of the story of Alexander Hamilton, one of America's founding fathers. Hamilton helped write the Constitution and was the first secretary of the United States Treasury and the architect of the American financial system. As Lin-Manuel put it, "This is a story about America then, told by America now."[2]

To say I loved **Hamilton** is an understatement. The songs, the ideas, the acting—can it get any better? I like to think God is constantly drawing our attention in a particular direction, but if you're like me, you might miss it the first time around. Or the second. But this wasn't my first time seeing the show; it was my third. And I was going to walk out of that theater as the final curtain fell having identified something I hadn't the first two times. And it would respark a mission.

Hamilton was a beast when it came to writing. Act 1 of **Hamilton** closes with a song called "Non-stop." When the Revolutionary War was over, Alexander Hamilton partnered up with John Jay and James Madison and between October 1787 and May 1788 wrote what came to be called the Federalist Papers. The total of eighty-five essays were published anonymously and for the purpose of defending the Constitution. John Jay wrote five, James Madison wrote twenty-nine, and Alexander Hamilton wrote fifty-one. The song "Non-stop" captures Hamilton's stubbornness and persistence. When the character Hamilton started singing the part about writing "like you're running out of time," I knew that God wanted me to hear something special.

> **How do you write like you're running out of time?**
> **Write day and night like you're running out of time?**
> **Every day you fight, like you're running out of time**
> **Like you're running out of time.**[3]

Those lyrics played in my head for the rest of the show but in a different way. I heard,

How do you live like you're running out of time?
Do you fight for people like you're running out of time?
How do you love Jesus like you're running out of time?
Do you live like you need Him to survive?

I am inspired by Hamilton's passion and his fire for pioneering revolutionary legislation and defending the cause of independence. This was a good cause—an important one, one that was historically necessary. But it's not a greater cause than the cause of Christ. Hamilton was fighting to defend the Constitution of the United States. We, as believers of the Truth, are fighting to shine light in darkness, to snatch people out of hell.

After the musical, my attention turned inward. I truly felt in the bottom of my heart a sense of urgency about how I was living my life, more than I ever had before. Centuries from now, are people going to be talking about my life, my choices, and my work with the same kind of passion? Would they say I cared about people? Would they point to the fact that I lived on purpose? It's not so much that I care about what others think or say about me but that I want my life and legacy to speak volumes about Christ's work for humanity and this dying world. And I want that message to be amplified by my mission-driven life for years to come.

If we truly believe in whose we are and know that people are hurting in a dark place, we must feel a sense of urgency to get to them and share with them faith, hope, and love. Does your life actually show a sense of urgency in what you believe?

If not, what might look different if it did?

Look Outside Yourself

Twenty-three-year-old Jaden Barr has had type 1 diabetes since he was fifteen years old, as well as reoccurring cholesteatoma, which has resulted in hearing loss in both ears. While he admits he has made mistakes and fallen short time and time again, Jaden aspires to live a life that glorifies God and make the most of the time he's been given.

I met Jaden in 2015 through our foundation's W15H program. I spent a few days with this amazing young man. We even had the chance to work out together. Part of my mission was to encourage him, but by the end of our time together, he was the one encouraging me! It's funny how God works that way so often.

"When you look outside yourself, that's where true mission is found."

In light of the health challenges Jaden has had to endure, he recognizes what it means to live a mission-possible life:

Without a clear mission, you're aimlessly going through life without intent or purpose. Experiencing firsthand the mission of the Tim Tebow Foundation has continually reminded me that God created me with a purpose: to know Him and to make Him known. It's easy to fall into the temptation of thinking life is about me and my plans, but I'm always reminded that the mission I've been given by God is much bigger and better than any worldly pursuit. By giving God control over my plans and following His instead, it makes the work I do have meaning and significance.

Right on, Jaden. This incredible young man truly has a heart that desires the greater things, what Jesus called "the good part" (Luke 10:42), or as the New Living Translation puts it, the "one thing worth being concerned about." And what exactly is that one thing? Pursuing God, sitting at His table, being in His presence without worry, fear, anxiety, résumé building, or winning a title. It's not that we never think about those things, but we don't let them dominate our vision. We strive and strain forward in this life with Jesus as our focus, with His will as our goal, and with His rewards as our prize.

Even at his young age, my friend Jaden has the wisdom to point out the dangers of me-centric living. This is tempting for all of us, no matter how young or old, no matter if you're a parent or a preacher, a student or a teacher, a web creator or a music maker. I love what Jaden once shared with me: "You'll end up empty if you make life or your mission about yourself. I feel most fulfilled and in line with my purpose when I'm looking outside of myself and my own desires and putting that energy into pouring into others. When you look outside yourself, that's where true mission is found."

Both Jaden and my engagement to Demi remind me of the power and passion that comes when you are focusing your energy outside of yourself. I want to live each day more alive and more passionate because of what Jesus has done for me. The past—His death and resurrection—keeps me motivated in the present to change the future. When you determine to live mission possible, rest assured you will not look back one day and wrestle with regret or painfully wonder what you did with your life.

When you get tired or overwhelmed or uncertain, don't forget the moment God changed your life. If you're reading this book right now and you don't know Him, that time can be now. Choose to trust Him in this very moment.

Don't forget the moment He challenged you to join the fight. And remember, you have a specific role to play in bringing faith, hope, and love to a world in need.

2

GOD POSSIBLE, PURPOSE POSSIBLE

Looking at them, Jesus said,
"With people it is impossible,
but not with God; for all things are
possible with God."
—MARK 10:27

A FEW YEARS AGO IN GHANA, AFRICA, a girl was born with spina bifida (which is a spinal birth defect) and bilateral clubfoot. Without choice, she was thrust into a culture where she was not wanted. People with special needs in Ghana, as in many countries, are marginalized and denied basic human rights. Often thought to be cursed or contagious, these children are used perversely in religious ceremonies, abandoned by their own parents, or even killed. But not this baby. She was loved and cared for by her mother. No one in their community understood why, and they were repulsed by what they considered undeserved affection.

When this girl was four, her mother died. Naked and alone, she was ignored by the people who lived in her community. To be clear, they knew she was there, alone and afraid, but they averted their eyes. They treated this orphaned child like a wild dog roaming the streets. In their perspective, the girl was better off dead. As each day passed without her being cared for, she grew weak and malnourished. Nearly a month later, she was found naked and deathly ill by a member of the social welfare office who arranged for the sick girl to be placed in a foster home. The people there knew that her life meant more than what others may have thought.

In Michigan that same year, Shannon and Cameron VanKoevering felt a call on their heart. They began to pray about adopting one or two boys, but something unsettled their prayers. They felt that God was telling them to wait. Later, they learned of a little girl in Ghana who needed surgery for spina bifida and bilateral clubfoot. The medical care this girl needed was complex and costly. The pull on this couple's hearts was evident, but they didn't have the money. They were hoping to adopt male siblings. Was this a God-ordained idea? How would it be possible?

Shannon and Cameron will always remember the day they first heard this little girl's name. It was Christabel, which means "beautiful Christian." In those melodic three syllables, this couple noticed a greater truth: Christ is able.

Not knowing how they would pay for the multiple surgeries and aftercare she required, the couple was understandably overwhelmed. Yet, remembering that Christ is able, they began contributing to her medical expenses. Little did they know the impact this precious little girl would have on their lives. Shannon says, "We fell in love with her beautiful smile, and while we felt 100 percent unqualified to parent a child with this type of disability, we jumped into the great unknown and let God take care of the details."

Two and a half years later—after grants, paperwork, a home study, interviews, appointments, and waiting, lots of waiting—the VanKoeverings finally welcomed Christabel to her forever family. Christabel has endured multiple surgeries to correct her feet. Barring a miracle, however, she will never be able to walk without assistance. Though this beautiful girl continues to struggle with vision problems and cognitive impairment, the VanKoeverings continue to trust God in His plan and with the details. They remain encouraged by the truth they first saw in their daughter: "Christ is able."

More Than You Can Handle

The year 2020 was overwhelming for most of us. A pandemic interrupted life as we knew it. We navigated a mandatory quarantine. Small businesses shut down, and many never reopened. We reached new levels of isolation and saw an uptick in physical and mental health issues. I think most of us had to wrangle and tame our feelings of uncertainty to function as best as we could. COVID-19 has made many people wish 2020 never happened to begin with. Refund, please!

How has your life been turned upside down? Maybe you took a big hit because of the pandemic, or maybe you did okay during that time. Maybe things are still hard. Maybe you are struggling with unruly everyday stuff. Many people didn't need a global crisis to learn what stress or worry or anxiety feels like. Life has a funny way of forcing us to navigate transitions, challenges, and disruptions all on its own.

The idea of living a mission-possible life can turn your stomach into knots for many reasons. While most of us want to tune in to God's purposes and the needs of others, those needs can overwhelm us. The VanKoeverings knew they wanted to adopt and understood, as well as they could, the challenges many adoptive parents face. When given the opportunity to give a forever home to Christabel, they hesitated, but not because they were selfish people or didn't want to welcome Christabel into their family. They hovered over the idea because the reality of the situation posed legitimate challenges. And yet Christ is able.

The prophet Jeremiah wrote, "Oh, Lord GOD!

Behold, You Yourself have made the heavens and the earth by Your great power and by Your outstretched arm! Nothing is too difficult for You" (Jeremiah 32:17). When Jeremiah wrote those confidence-charged words, he was in prison—not because he had stolen a neighbor's tractor or embezzled money, but because he spoke the truth. The ancient prophet foretold that the people of Israel would be captured and defeated by the Chaldeans. He also mentioned that the king of Israel would be captured. So, as you might imagine, this prophecy enraged King Zedekiah. With a bruised ego, the king did what he had to do to make himself feel better about the whole situation. He tossed Jeremiah in the courtyard prison, a place of temporary confinement where the prophet was imprisoned but given some freedom. Jeremiah was allowed to continue his prophetic ministry and conduct certain business transactions.

When we make the decision to trust Him with our lives, we are automatically seated at the table of the humanly impossible.

As the prophecy begins to unfold and Israel unravels into a war zone, Jeremiah's cousin visits him in prison. He doesn't bring cupcakes or an inspirational book or pictures from his family that the prophet can tack to his jail-cell wall. Instead, he proposes a real estate transaction. The cousin asks Jeremiah if he wants to buy his land. I may not be Jeff Bezos, but I can tell you that it already sounds like a ridiculous idea (no offense, Jeremiah's cousin). Plus, the plot of land he wants to sell is in an area that had already been seized by the Chaldeans. The area was in ruins. On the surface, this was a ludicrous offer. Surely, Jeremiah would not want to buy property in a war zone while he was in jail. But here's the kicker. Being a prophet, Jeremiah had already been warned by God that the cousin would show up to make such an offer, so when it happened, he wasn't surprised. He was more like, "Okay, cool, God. As always, You were right. Let's buy this land!" The prophet gets the money together and makes the transaction, complete with a notary public and witnesses and signed-and-sealed documents placed in a clay pot.

See, as strange as the query sounded, God knew something. Even though the nation of Israel would be defeated at the hands of their enemy, their land would eventually become their own again. He assures the prophet by saying, "Houses and fields and vineyards will again be purchased in this land" (verse 15). Years later, the dust would settle, and the people of Israel would be free to return home.

Jeremiah is choosing to believe that God's promises will come to pass. It's an investment in faith.

At the same time that Jeremiah pens verse 17, proclaiming that nothing is too hard for God, he is struggling a bit with buyer's remorse. Can you blame the guy? He's the proud owner of a field that is being trampled by soldiers who spill the blood of Israel. Plus, he's sitting in prison without an official release date. Trying to manage a property behind bars in the middle of a war has got to be brutal.

After Jeremiah prays for understanding, the God of the impossible repeats His assurance:

Behold, I am going to gather them out of all the lands to which I have driven them in My anger, in My wrath, and in great indignation; and I will bring them back to this place and have them live in safety. They shall be My people, and I will be their God; and I will give them one heart and one way, so that they will fear Me always, for their own good and for the good of their children after them. I will make an everlasting covenant with them that I will not turn away from them, to do them good; and I will put the fear of Me in their hearts, so that they will not turn away from Me. . . . Just as I brought all this great disaster on this people, so I am going to bring on them all the good that I am promising them. . . . For I will restore their fortunes. (verses 37–40, 42, 44)

In other words, "Jeremiah, I got this. I know this ordeal seems hard and maybe even impossible. I know it makes no sense. And while I won't tell you how or when, I **will** restore what will be taken away. You have My word. Trust Me—I know something you don't."

The movie **Elf** tells us that smiling is main character Buddy's favorite thing. I like to think that one of God's favorite things is intervening in the impossible.

God has a habit of making His presence known or intervening in impossible missions. It seems as if He's drawn to predicaments for which no plan B or Z exists. If it can't be done in the natural, if it can't be figured out by the efforts of humans alone, if it's a problem without a solution, it's the perfect venue for God to do His best work.

The anchor of the gospel rests in the truth that we cannot save ourselves by our pedigrees, good works, or impressive career histories. We receive the free gift of salvation through what Jesus has done for us on the cross. This is one of the reasons the Son of God said, "The things that are impossible with people are possible with God" (Luke 18:27).

When we make the decision to trust Him with our lives, we are automatically seated at the table of the humanly impossible. It's not about what we can do; it's about what God can do through us.

The VanKoeverings didn't have the knowledge, background, or finances to adopt a girl with special needs. But God did. He had everything they needed. And in their hearts, they chose to trust and believe that God "is able to do far more abundantly beyond all that we ask or think, according to the power that works within us" (Ephesians 3:20).

> **When our willingness collides with God's power, an inconceivable unfolding of purpose erupts.**

Do you think Moses felt confident when God asked him to lead a million weary and frazzled people out of Egypt through a sea and on foot, all while being chased by a massive army of soldiers? Doubt it. Think about the handful of senior-citizen couples in the Bible who had babies well after being eligible for Medicare. Do you think Abraham and Sarah and Elizabeth and Zechariah just happened to be super-fit keto-nuts with twenty-something-year-old insides? What about Joshua, the leader of Israel who won a battle after God made the sun stand still (see Joshua 10:1–15)? Was that a cosmic phenomenon that happens only once every billion years? Was it something that Joshua expected would happen? Of course not. When our willingness collides with God's power, an inconceivable unfolding of purpose erupts.

Get Overwhelmed by God's Spirit

Are you overwhelmed today? Maybe you're confused as to where to begin your mission. Maybe you feel as though you can barely handle life, let alone a mission-driven one. Take a breath with me. I want to remind you that even if you feel incapable or insufficient, God has everything you need so you can do what He has put on your heart. You are in the right place at the right time.

Instead of feeling overwhelmed by what seems impossible, imagine being overwhelmed by the Spirit of God. Shift your focus, even just a little bit. When Jesus rose from the dead and was taken to heaven, He promised His disciples that although He would not be with them in body any longer, He would send the Holy Spirit to strengthen and comfort them. The only way to experience the active power of God in our lives is to be filled with the Holy Spirit (see Ephesians 5:18). Let's dive a little deeper here. What does it mean to be filled with the Spirit?

According to Bible commentary by author Max Anders,

Some interpreters equate this command with instances of being filled with the Spirit in the Book of Acts in which miraculous things happened: people spoke in tongues; prophecies and visions were given; people were healed. "Be filled" in this verse (**plarao**) is not the same word as the one used in the Book of Acts (**pimplemi**). . . . In this ethical context, it means directed, influenced, and ultimately governed by the Holy Spirit. . . .

This filling, then, is best understood, as a command for the believer to yield himself to the illuminating, convicting, and empowering work of the Holy Spirit. As he works in our hearts through his Word, our lives are brought into conformity with the will of God.[1]

All Christ followers have God's Spirit living in them, but not all Christ followers live filled or controlled by the Spirit's power. The Spirit never leaves us, but when we are disobedient, our sinful behavior can limit the active work of God in our lives. On the other hand, when we obey God's commands/ will, we can expect to see the Spirit's fruit in our lives. This is an ongoing work as we humble ourselves before God.

If you are a believer, He is with you. He is your constant companion. His presence in your life is a nonnegotiable. It's pretty crazy, isn't it? The Spirit of God living on the inside of you, filling you with power? That's what makes God's plan for your life possible!

Job 33:4 tells us, "The Spirit of God has made me, and the breath of the Almighty gives me life." Take a minute right now to meditate on that truth. What does that passage of Scripture mean to you? What kind of hope ignites in your heart? Does it bring some relief?

Settle yourself into that verse. Read it slowly, savoring each syllable:

"The Spirit of God has made me,

And the breath of the Almighty gives me life."

Trade the anxiety, the dread, or the pressure that weighs heavily on your heart for the refreshing truth that God breathes life into you. He doesn't feed you with fear. He doesn't drown you in guilt. He won't force you to do something you can't do without Him. If He is prompting you to do something, He will equip, empower, and encourage you and see that mission to completion.

Here's another truth that can alleviate some of the pressure you feel. I've had many conversations with people who feel the mission they are called to is well beyond their abilities. It's too big. One person can't end homelessness. One person can't ensure that every child has adequate nutrition. One person can't make clean water a global reality. This is logical. But mission-possible living doesn't depend on the completion of these large goals. You just do what you can, with what you got, for the glory of God. For example, my dad's mission is to preach the gospel to every person in the Philippines, but my dad can't change someone's heart. That's God's job. That's the role of the Holy Spirit. My dad is committed to doing his part and leaves the rest to God.

Take a Step and Let God Do the Rest

Though we at the foundation had been serving in anti-human-trafficking efforts for seven years, in 2020 I thought about going public with it. I asked the opinions of a few people I trusted. Some thought it was too risky. Others said it didn't fit our brand. One person wondered how it was even possible to shine light on something so dark. It seemed dangerous. I didn't have answers, but I couldn't shake the feeling that God was calling me in that direction. I didn't assume my work would completely end human trafficking. I can't do that in my own strength and power. But I could do my part and engage in a solution in some way and watch God turn what seemed impossible into the possible.

I'd like to share the story of one woman who encouraged me with the knowledge that no matter how dark a situation, light can somehow find a way to shine forth.

Natalie, whose name has been changed to protect her privacy, was sold for sex beginning when she was four or five years old. She and her family lived in a small camper in a rural area with no electricity or running water. Her parents were addicted to drugs and would sell their children for sex at night in order to supply their drug habit. Natalie struggled in school and was consistently rejected because she was dirty and unkempt. She actually got in trouble at school for wearing the same dirty clothes every day and shoes without laces. Natalie wonders if her life might have turned out better if teachers had known she needed someone to help her. She was removed from her home by social services on several occasions, but she was always brought back and continued being sold for sex until the end of her high school years.

Natalie graduated from high school and even earned a college scholarship with the help of a caring teacher. But by this time, she suffered from depression, anxiety, PTSD, and dissociation. Although she was intelligent, Natalie could not keep up with the demands of her classes due to the grief, loss, and emotional pain her family continued to inflict upon her. So, two years into her college career, she enlisted in the military in order to get away from her family, whom she knew would continue to drain her of any resources she could pull together. Natalie excelled briefly in the military but soon was put on mental health leave due to severe depression making her unable to fully function. She eventually lost her job, leaving her homeless and living out of her car with just her dog and military gear.

Eventually, she ran out of money and gas, alone and scared. It was there that she was noticed by two older men who showed sympathy to her dilemma. She was promised a room, food, a shower, and that they would put gas in her car and bring it to their house, as well as needed support to get her on her feet. It all sounded too good to be true. They told her she could even bring her dog with her. The two men took her to a modest home in a middle-class neighborhood and moved her into her very own room.

Then they drilled the door shut. They starved her. They didn't give her any food, nor did they allow her to go to the bathroom or use the shower. She was sold for sex to anyone willing to buy. After months of this existence, Natalie was let out of her room for just a moment or two one day, just to get a sandwich. Her sellers assumed she was too weak to run, but fighting for her life and freedom, she tried to escape. She didn't get far and collapsed in the driveway. Thankfully, a neighbor saw her and called 911. Natalie was admitted to a hospital, where she recovered and was identified by a social worker as a trafficking victim. Natalie was able to find hope and healing with our amazing team of loving counselors and the team at Her Song, a faith-based organization that engages women in healing body, mind, and spirit in a safe community and a place to belong.

Today, Natalie, now thirty years old, supports herself and her dog. She is free. Natalie has finished her associate degree and works at the same hospital that identified her as a trafficking victim. Actually, no, a trafficking survivor. She's still there today, using her nursing skills to help others while she finishes her degree.

I want to fight for girls and boys like Natalie and even to prevent them from ending up in that terrible situation. The road is long and hard, but I'm committed to staying in the fight and allowing God to do what He wants.

> **Living a mission-possible life is not about growing our self-confidence; it's about expanding our God-confidence.**

Our mission is not to end all evil. If it were, we would have every right to feel overwhelmed. As long as we exist on this earth, the Enemy will continue to prowl throughout like a roaring lion. We don't have the power to end every pain and hurt in this world. But our mission is to honor God as we make a difference wherever and however we can. The outcome, the result, the stories—we don't have control over all those things.

Don't rest your confidence on your ability or the longevity of your passion or your singular branding. Living a mission-possible life is not about growing our self-confidence; it's about expanding our God-confidence.

Express Confidence

When COVID-19 shut down the country, I was supposed to be on a baseball diamond in Port St.

Lucie for spring training. I know that seems silly compared to the massive loss of life. Most of us took a hit from the pandemic. Some have lost loved ones; others have lost opportunities. Like many people whose plans got intercepted or dismantled, I was disappointed. I'm not going to lie—it really bummed me out. At the same time, it was a perfect opportunity to trust in God's plan for my life. Over the years, I've learned it's easy to trust when you're winning championships, when everyone loves you, and when you're scoring touchdowns or slugging home runs. But when your reality is less than your ideal, it is harder to believe that God has it all under control. Disappointments chip away at our confidence.

But we can find joy and purpose in even the darkest places. That's not only something the apostle Paul wrote; it's something he lived. Paul wrote the book of Philippians to a group of people he loved—people he considered family. Philippians is a pretty cheery book. Paul didn't have to get on them for quarreling over who should eat what and when and how as he did in the book of Romans. Instead, this letter overflows with peppy encouragement. You know, the kind of Scripture we love to quote and post on social media and coffee cups.

"For I am confident of this very thing, that He who began a good work among you will complete it by the day of Christ Jesus" (1:6).

"For to me, to live is Christ, and to die is gain" (1:21).

And we can't forget one of the most well-known scriptures, which you'll find in most middle school locker rooms—in Christian ones, at least. "I can do all things through Him who strengthens me" (4:13).

Don't you get pumped up just reading those words? I bet if Paul were around today, he'd get flooded with invites to speak at conferences all over the world. The irony is that he was writing these encouraging words from prison. Some scholars say that he was actually holed up in the basement of a prison where the sewage system was. It was dark, it was dirty, and it stank. And as the odor of human waste and rotten food saturated the air, Paul wrote words that strengthened and emboldened the spirit of the church in Philippi.

I love how he launched the fourth chapter: "Rejoice in the Lord always; again I will say, rejoice!" (verse 4). The word **rejoice** isn't one I use often in my vernacular. I doubt you do either. When's the last time you said to a friend, "What a beautiful day! Let's rejoice together!"? Never, right? While spending time in my NIV study Bible, I came across a footnote that made more sense to me. It substituted "expressing confidence in" for "rejoice in."[2] Expressing confidence made a lot of sense to me.

While imprisoned and facing the possibility of being killed for his faith at any moment, Paul could have written about how anxious, worried, and afraid he was. Instead, he chose to record an expression of his unshakable confidence in God, which he wanted other believers to share in.

In a time of fear and panic, I want to be someone who expresses confidence in God. I also want this to be true when life doesn't seem seamless. I need to be confident in God when I'm launching a mission that I'm certain I can't fulfill in my own power. I want to express confidence in God when uncertainty holds me in its grip. I want to express confidence in God when I'm tired because every little thing that can go wrong does. I want to express confidence in God's plan for me when I feel overwhelmed with the details and lose sight of the vision.

I love how **The Message** paraphrases verses 4–5: "Celebrate God all day, every day. I mean, **revel** in him! Make it as clear as you can to all you meet that you're on their side, working with them and not against them. Help them see that the Master is about to arrive. He could show up any minute!"

This passage of Scripture demands our celebration and speaks of the same type of urgency that I had been reminded of when I watched **Hamilton** for the third time. I'm not guaranteeing your mission-possible journey is going to be easy, but I have a feeling you already know it won't be. You've done some hard things and have seen God's faithfulness in pretty messy and painful seasons.

Don't stop trusting Him when it's dark, dank, and smelly. Don't give up the mission because you don't fully understand it and can't figure out the game plan. When your doubt begins to rumble, remember what God has done in the past. Express your confidence that He has a plan and a purpose for your life. You are not a man or woman who quits; you are a conqueror through the work Jesus did on the cross. Stop focusing on what you can't do, and remember that nothing is too hard for God.

Nothing.

3

RIGHT WHERE YOU ARE

**Do what you can, with what
you've got, where you are.**

—A FRIEND OF THEODORE ROOSEVELT

WHAT'S THE FIRST THING THAT POPS
into your head when I mention the words **mission-
possible life**? Do you think of a speaker sharing
about Jesus? Or how about a missionary rejecting
first-world luxuries and choosing to live in a re-
mote village without Wi-Fi or indoor plumbing
to share the gospel with people from other parts of
the world? On one hand, yes, those are certainly
mission-possible vocations. On the other hand, liv-
ing out mission is more holistic and less dramatic
than you might imagine.

Martin Luther wrote, "The idea that service to
God should have only to do with a church altar,

singing, reading, sacrifice, and the like is without doubt but the worst trick of the devil. . . . The whole world could abound with services to the Lord . . . not only in churches but also in the home, kitchen, workshop, and field."[1]

Being a mission-possible Christian has less to do with holding a religious vocation and more to do with developing an intimate relationship with Jesus. Mission stems from embracing our identity in Him. When we deepen our walk with Jesus, He invades every part of our lives. He doesn't become real only at a church service, small-group meeting, or worship event. We are image bearers of God on the field, in the boardroom, and in our kitchens. Each minute. Each day. Every day.

> **When you begin to live beyond the surface of what you see, you begin to transcend the ordinary.**

Whatever you are tasked with in the everyday—even what you believe is the most trivial of duties or responsibilities, or a boring job you are always complaining about—find a way to invite purpose into that space. What can you do to make someone's life better after he or she has interacted with you? How can you approach a challenge you've been avoiding knowing God is on your side? If you're changing diapers or teaching kindergarten in a virtual setting or folding sweatshirts in retail, think about what you could be doing differently or doing more of (or less of) that unveils whose you are. When you begin to live beyond the surface of what you see, you begin to transcend the ordinary.

To All the Miss Nancys in the World

One thing the church I attended growing up was known for was its theatrical productions of faith-based musicals. We're talking as "big and wow" as Broadway. Hundreds of people in the cast. A full orchestra. Live animals. Incredible sets and costumes. Thousands would attend, and even more would tune in when it was broadcast on television.

I loved watching these plays, but I never wanted to be in them. I wasn't comfortable speaking in public. It wasn't that I hated it; I just wasn't confident. My parents took notice of this early on and did what good parents do: they made me do it. They signed me up for any activity in which I needed to stand in front of a crowd and talk, even sing. That's right, sing. Mom and Dad made me pray out loud in front of others. They forced me to give presentations at science fairs. And then they encouraged me to do my favorite thing in the world as a kid: audition for church plays (note my sarcasm). That was the worst. I would much rather do a hundred push-ups or throw a ball to showcase my skills for a part. And, yes, I realize that a performance of strength and speed doesn't really fit into the plot of Noah's story.

I remember one of my first auditions. Seven- or eight-year-old Tim Tebow stood on the center of a huge platform, staring into the eyes of multiple judges and a few others who were seated in the grand auditorium. The judges, void of facial expression, were ready to assess if I was up to the task of being cast in the play. I kept squinting, my vision blurred by a blaring spotlight shining the light on my talent (or, rather, exposing my inadequacy—however you want to spin it). Like the rest of the candidates, I was supposed to introduce my performance by stating my name, my age, my grade, and a favorite quote, such as a Bible verse. Can't really screw that up, right? I stated my name but forgot to mention my age and grade because I was so nervous.

The second I cleared my throat and heard the scratchy sound blast through the microphone and ricochet from the space around me back to my ears, my body began to tremble. Eyes fixed on my feet, I mumbled some poem my parents made me memorize—that was my quote. I don't know if the judges could even hear or understand a word I said. Staring down at my shoelaces, I gulped a deep breath, trying to psych myself up for the next worst thing. I had to sing. If you haven't heard me sing, there's a good reason I was on **Lip Sync Battle** and not **American Idol.** It's not a talent God gifted me with. Dying for this moment of humiliation to end,

I rushed through "Jesus Loves Me," which I chose since it was the easiest song I could remember. Every sound that leaped from my throat fumbled out of pitch. When I was done squawking the last line, I speed-walked to the side curtain and regained my composure. Relief swept over me. Though I was uncomfortable every second of standing on that stage, I was proud I had done it.

Somehow I got a part in the play. I was chosen to play a camel's butt. Let that sink in for a minute. The genesis of my theatrical experience literally started at the bottom.

At the time, I was finally eligible—agewise, at least—to sign up for the church choir. Obviously, Mom and Dad were delighted. I definitely did not share their enthusiasm. But I would soon meet my choir teacher, Miss Nancy, who would leave such a positive lasting impression on me as a kid that I was honored to be able to invite her to Demi's and my wedding about two decades later. Over the years and still today, whenever I think about her or mention her name, I can't help but smile and feel grateful.

I remained under the tutelage of Miss Nancy from second grade through fifth grade. Although I started out as a camel's butt, by the time I had graduated elementary school, I performed in the last few plays as a Supreme Court justice and Superman. That's quite an impressive progression over a few years.

I may have been basically taking up space in choir due to my lack of talent, but I was happy to do my best for this special teacher. Miss Nancy had a gift. More than one, actually. But it wasn't just that she was a great teacher who had remarkable musical talent. She was passionate about her position. She used what she was doing and where she was planted to make a difference. Miss Nancy cared about the students. And she made every one of us feel special, even the kids who couldn't carry a tune past the first three notes. Like me.

What I especially loved about her was how she flipped what I had considered awful into something fun. It wasn't her skill that made this happen; it was the place in her heart she taught from. Miss Nancy's spirit was steeped in joy, from the smile that always glowed on her face, to her positive attitude, to her words of encouragement to all students—the ones who had talent and the ones who were better at other things. Even the teachers who worked with her, like Miss Tammy, shared her passion. Let me be clear that my dislike of choir and singing didn't change. If I could sing, I would have loved it, but I sucked. It was my admiration for Miss Nancy and her team that made me want to do more than just stand there and mouth some lyrics. My teacher created an environment that grew musical gifts and drew out the best in her students. It's what I saw her do with excellence, and it's what made me consider her one of my favorites.

Unlike some teachers, Miss Nancy didn't look at

me as a one-sided jock or give me a hard time when I had to miss a rehearsal because I had a game. To me that was a huge deal. I can't tell you how many times teachers and even leaders at church would make clear their disdain because I'd miss or be late to a service or an event due to a game. Not Miss Nancy. Sometimes she'd even let me get a rehearsal in before a game or practice. And she always asked how it went. That's genuine care right there, and it's something I'll never forget. I may not have shown a shred of theatrical stardom, but I truly enjoyed the plays she put on twice a year—so much so that when I got older, I invited the teammates on my travel team to see the productions. A few of them even made the decision to trust in Jesus because of these events! This never would have happened if it weren't for Miss Nancy.

I was so influenced by Miss Nancy's passion and her mission-possible life that right after I won the Heisman, I went back to play Goliath in one of the shows. That's how much I respected and appreciated my teacher. And if she asked me to sing for her today, I'd grab a mic and belt out whatever she wanted, no doubt.

There are great teachers who bless our lives like Miss Nancy, who say or do things you'll never forget. But it's not just teachers who do this. It's the moms and dads who hug their kids close and cry with them when Mufasa dies in **The Lion King.**

It's the man or woman who remembers the name of the barista who serves them every morning. It's the coach who cares more about character than scores. Wherever we are, in whatever we are doing, we can always do something to transcend what can start out as seemingly insignificant.

Whatever You Do

As I look back at the life of Jesus, I realize something: He lived fully with purpose in every moment. This was true when He spoke to a crowd of thousands, when He breathed life into a stranger in an act of social suicide, when He swapped jokes with little kids, and when He broke bread with His besties. In all these things, Jesus was pleasing His father (see John 8:29). Why? Because He lived each day present and aware and fueled by intentional action. Wherever He went, His purpose didn't stop, even when He'd spend time in solitude to pray. He offered forgiveness to the shamed. He fed those who were hungry. He paid attention to those who had been forgotten or ignored. He loved the last, the least, and the lost. Those are all actions we can imitate no matter how many followers we have.

When we compartmentalize our lives, we do ourselves a disservice. We don't honor God by moving the kingdom forward only on certain days of the week or times of the day. We have the honor of living in such a way that, as Jesus observed, we can please our Father in heaven in whatever we do.

The Bible teaches this very principle. Ecclesiastes 9:10 tells us, "Whatever your hand finds to do, do it with all your might." The apostle Paul, who was known for his devotion to Christ and his positive attitude even in the worst of circumstances, wrote, "Whether you eat or drink, or whatever you do, do all things for the glory of God" (1 Corinthians 10:31).

He gave the same directive in the third chapter of Colossians:

> Whatever you do in word or deed, do everything in the name of the Lord Jesus, giving thanks through Him to God the Father. . . . Whatever you do, do your work heartily, as for the Lord and not for people, knowing that it is from the Lord that you will receive the reward of the inheritance. It is the Lord Christ whom you serve. (verses 17, 23–24)

In these passages, Paul is giving Christians a genuine command. What he's saying is that in all things, no matter what, turn your present task, moment, or emotion into an act of worship. Rather than being motivated by temporary pleasure, affirmation, or earthly reward, maintain a pure servant's heart before the Lord. Our attitudes are reflections of our souls. Our actions and motives should derive from who we represent. When we wholeheartedly align ourselves under this intention, our energy and effort will be well received by others. However, the God of the universe is who we should ultimately seek to please.

> **Ecclesiastes 9:10 tells us, "Whatever your hand finds to do, do it with all your might."**

In five separate letters (1 Corinthians, Galatians, Ephesians, Colossians, and 1 Thessalonians), Paul speaks of working for the Lord from the sincerity of our hearts and not for men. This was a critical issue he wanted to communicate to early believers. I'm guessing Paul's emphasis came from what Jesus said was the utmost important command in Mark 12:30: "Love the LORD your God with all your heart, and with all your soul, and with all your mind, and with all your strength."

What is it you do? Do you teach? Do you take out the trash and fold laundry? Do you chauffeur your kids to practices and games? Do you lead a small group? Do you negotiate high-stake deals? Are you given a regular paycheck to do something you love or something you can't stand? Do you have a side hustle? Are you learning a new trade? Do you write songs? Have you finished your first book?

Whatever you do, do it with all your might. If you don't, you are not valuing the time that God gave you. You're telling Him that gift is not worth it. You may not be happy with where you are, but He can still pull purpose through it. You can have ambition to be somewhere better or do something else and strive toward those things, but never forget God can and, if you are willing, will use you wherever you are in the process.

Purpose is intertwined in every area of your life. Even though TTF is so important to me, guess what? I still have speaking engagements for many other nonprofit organizations. My purpose doesn't have borders. Even though I can't share the gospel while working on **SEC Nation** or **First Take,** I can still have joy and passion and purpose in what I do and ask people how they are and genuinely care about their answers. Purpose. Being on those television shows is not my calling, but when I'm there, my purpose doesn't cease to matter.

You may be in a role or situation that is not the entire expression of your purpose, but you are still meant to carry your purpose into those places.

There's power in allowing God to manifest His presence in whatever you do, right here and right now. One way to do this is to take pride in all the work you do, whether it's in a boardroom, throwing a baseball on the field, or caring for little ones in your home.

Mission Excellence

In 605 BC, King Nebuchadnezzar of the Babylonian empire had invaded Israel and taken captive its men, women, and children. It would be seventy years before these kidnapped people would return to their homeland.

Daniel and his buddies were among the people chosen for a specialized government training program. They were smart, good looking, strong, and young, likely between the ages of eleven and eighteen. This opportunity came with some serious drawbacks. Sure, they weren't handcuffed or thrown into a dirty prison cell without food or water. But still, they were captives, and not a day went by when they weren't reminded of this bleak reality.

But Daniel's captivity was also an opportunity. Another prophet, by the name of Jeremiah, had prophesied this very event. Jeremiah also gave some encouragement the exiles could lean into. "Build houses and live in them; and plant gardens and eat their produce. . . . Seek the prosperity of the city where I have sent you into exile, and pray to the LORD in its behalf; for in its prosperity will be your prosperity" (Jeremiah 29:5, 7). In other words, make yourselves at home, because you're going to be here for a while.

So, Daniel transformed a kidnapping into a mission. He had been handpicked for this three-year

training program that would create diplomats
of sorts who would one day serve the nation of
Babylon. Daniel learned the language and was edu-
cated in their history, customs, and culture. He was
obedient throughout his forced service, though he
did not forget his spiritual heritage. In one of his
first acts of standing up for his beliefs, Daniel made
a deal with his supervisor: Instead of indulging in
the Babylonian cuisine, perhaps he and his Israelite
buddies could follow the diet of their origin (veg-
gies and water) for ten days and then his boss could
decide which group fared better. Daniel's supervisor
agreed, and after ten days had passed, the man was
stunned. The Babylonian trainees came out of the
ten-day plan sporting dad bods and needing naps.
Daniel and his team of men came out energized and
buff. This test gave Daniel an edge. His superior was
so impressed, he allowed the would-be prophet and
his friends to eat what they preferred.

When training was complete, Daniel and his
friends were promoted to positions of power.
During that time, King Darius had succeeded
King Nebuchadnezzar, and while King Darius
liked Daniel, he mandated some devastating po-
lices, particularly to God-serving Israelites. One
law demanded that all people were to pray to no
one except the king. When Daniel was found pray-
ing to God, he was punished: death by lions. No
worries, though. God sent an angel to literally shut

the mouth of these ravenous monsters. The mangy-haired beasts couldn't even roar properly, and Daniel was released unscathed.

But before we see him come out on top and shock the king and the guards who pushed him into the pit, the Bible tells another (earlier) story about his character. Daniel was one of three who were appointed to oversee 120 satraps, chief representatives of the king. Daniel was good at his job. Really good. The Bible tells us, "This Daniel began distinguishing himself among the commissioners and satraps because he possessed an extraordinary spirit, and the king intended to appoint him over the entire kingdom" (Daniel 6:3). Wow! The king was going to give Daniel the keys to the Babylonian kingdom.

I imagine this promotion came with some benefits, such as better health insurance and more vacation days. It also came with some enemies. As Daniel proved himself an excellent leader, those around him started turning an ugly shade of green. How could this lowly Israelite sprint up the ladder so fast and be charged with such authority and power? It wasn't fair. And it was quite a blow to their egos. These men calculated a way that would surely burst their colleague's happy bubble (insert evil laughter). They hired top-notch investigators to find and expose the skeletons in Daniel's closet. Maybe he had a string of mistresses or was bingeing on Oreos when no one was looking. But there was no dirt to be found. Not even a hint of indiscretion.

"And no negligence or corruption was to be found in him" (verse 4).

We can learn a lot from the life of Daniel. He fought for excellence. He worked and studied and trained hard. He went the extra mile. He showed up early and stayed late. He wasn't satisfied just to get by. He wanted to do more. This pursuit was inherent in his spirit. It was a part of his DNA. He was a great illustration of how Ecclesiastes 9:10 tells us to follow God's leading.

I love the SEC slogan "It just means more." It reminds me of how Daniel lived his life. Miss Nancy too. A job wasn't just a job. For these two people, their employment meant more than just waiting for the semimonthly direct deposit to hit their bank accounts. They transcended their roles in ways that brought joy and purpose to their lives and the lives of others. I realize you may not have found your dream job. Maybe you don't want to stay an editor your whole life and you long to write your own book one day. Maybe you're tired of putting in long hours at the firm and desire to spend more time with your family. It's hard to strive for excellence when you're not happy. Doing so is not something that comes naturally, but it is possible. It's a decision you'll need to make for yourself.

If you choose to approach your job with disdain or even apathy, two things happen. One, you don't please God. Two, you are not giving yourself the best chance of finding a better opportunity, whether in that same place of employment or elsewhere. Be the person you want others to see. Take pride in your work. Be attentive. Find solutions instead of complaining. Take time to think about what intentional choices you can make to cultivate life out of what may be a boring or stressful or rote job.

Living a mission-possible life means watering and fertilizing and cultivating the ground where you are planted, even if it seems nothing more than a wasteland. I love what Jesus said in Luke 16:10: "The one who is faithful in a very little thing is also faithful in much; and the one who is unrighteous in a very little thing is also unrighteous in much." I try to look for such faithfulness in the people who work with me. If I see someone who is faithful and doing a great job with smaller assignments, I take notice. Recently, I interviewed four potential employees for the foundation. I didn't ask them questions about their skills. I had read their résumés, so I already knew where they went to school and where they last worked. I focused my questions on investigating if they had the ability to learn, grow, and adapt. I don't need perfect employees who don't make mistakes; I need people around me who are willing to be stretched, constantly learn, and grow. These are people who strive to be better tomorrow than they already are today.

The way I see it, there are three practical ways to live a mission-possible life with the excellence that Daniel modeled for us.

1. Do It with Integrity, Even If No One Is Watching

As I was growing up, my parents created a rewards program for us five kids called Daddy's Dollars. Every time someone outside our family complimented our character, Dad would give us a dollar. Sometimes he'd give us a real bill, other times a printed paper we could exchange for a prize in a chest of goodies or for privileges, such as TV or computer time. We would also get dollars for doing extra chores. My family is extremely competitive. It didn't matter if we were playing Monopoly or basketball—we would hustle and duke it out and do everything in our power to win. Even as the youngest of five, I was determined to get the most Daddy's Dollars out of everyone, so I worked hard for compliments. I helped carry groceries. I always held the door open for someone. I was first to raise my hand to volunteer. And I did most of these things in front of my parents, on purpose, so they could see how awesome I was and give me a buck. And that was the problem.

Eventually, I realized how empty it was to do nice things for a dollar or a pat on the back or any other material reward. I remembered one of the Bible verses I memorized growing up: "The ways of everyone are before the eyes of the LORD, and He observes all his paths" (Proverbs 5:21). God is always watching us. He sees us doing the right thing, the wrong thing, and nothing. Who are you when no one is watching? Do you do the right thing because it's simply the right thing to do? I can guarantee that when we start living and acting as though God's eyes are always watching, we will start living a little differently. And even if no one notices that you swept up the store or organized the file system without being asked or spent two hours after your shift was over to help the new employee get adjusted, it doesn't matter. While it's nice to be rewarded with stuff, it's more fulfilling to please our heavenly Father.

2. Do It with a Heart of Gratitude

There were many times as a professional athlete when I wasn't crazy about an outcome. Getting cut, for instance. It stung every time. And although I was crazy-blessed outside of football, it was easy to feel bitter at not getting something I'd worked so hard for. I've learned the importance of flipping my mentality and choosing gratitude every time. It's so easy to turn off the sweet melody of being grateful when we find ourselves in a funk or grumpy for what we may think is a pretty good reason.

I don't know about you, but for me it can happen every now and then in a split second on an ordinary Sunday afternoon. I could have a superspiritual morning at church, fun time with family and friends at brunch, but then, while watching a quarterback play in an NFL game and listening to announcers make a passing comment about something he may not have done so well, get a little twisted thinking about how those same commentators would have verbally bashed my head in on the same play. And all of a sudden I forget about the great worship experience from a few hours earlier or how good I felt hanging with my mom and munching on good steak. I sulk, and if I am not aware and refuse to do anything about it, I stay anchored in that ugly place. I have to be mindful of what I'm feeling. I have to think about what I'm thinking about. And I have to choose to think about what God has done in my life and how faithful He is. It may take time to remedy my poor attitude, but I commit to choosing gratitude. It's funny what happens when I shift to being grateful. Everything changes. I find myself smiling more. The muscles in my neck relax, and the headache that sprang up on me dissipates. I don't snap at people. I become more patient with my wife. And then I'm in a much better mood (though I still disagree with the critics).

There is much to say about the regular practice of gratitude. The benefits are many. For one, being grateful improves a person's physical health. A study conducted by psychologists at the University of Miami observed a group of subjects. A third of them were asked to keep a daily journal of all the things that happened that they were grateful for. Another third of subjects were asked to write down the events that happened that irritated them. The final group of subjects were asked to record daily events without specifically either a positive or negative description. At the end of the ten-week study, in comparison to the other two groups, the group that practiced gratitude felt more optimistic and positive about life, were more physically active, and had fewer visits to the doctor.[2] There are many studies that include similar findings. Gratitude improves relationships, correlates to better moods, and reduces the risk of heart failure. You may not feel like it, but there's always a reason to be grateful. Even right now, thank God for the very breath you are breathing and His presence that is within you this very moment.

3. Do It with Excellence

Aim to be and even top your personal best. If you're a barista, do your job with excellence. If you're a full-time parent, be intentional in how you raise and lead your children. If you're a student, study, study, and study some more. If you're an athlete, train and keep training. If you manage a company, set high standards and teach your employees how they can meet them. Make an effort. Put in the work.

Your Work Is Worship

In the Hebrew word **avad,** three ideas converge to form a unique relationship. In the Old Testament, the word is used to express the English concepts of work, worship, or service (note the italicized words in the following scriptures):

A person goes out to his work and to his **labor** [avad] until evening. (Psalm 104:23)

As for me and my house, we will **serve** [avad] the LORD. (Joshua 24:15)

The LORD said to Moses, "Go to Pharaoh and say to him, 'This is what the LORD says: Let my people go, so that they may **worship** [avad] me.'" (Exodus 8:1, NIV)

See, the ancient Hebrews integrated these three words in one. Though **avad** wasn't their primary word for "worship," they still understood that their work and service acted as worship to God. Even in the New Testament, Paul makes this parallel in Romans 12:1.[3]

Living a mission-possible life, in whatever our hands find to do, is an act of worship.

A mission-possible life must be shaped by **avad.** God has integrated our relationship with Him into the everyday. Our faith walks affect everything we do. We worship God when we scramble eggs for our little ones. We worship when we visit our elderly neighbors who hardly get visitors anymore. We worship when we study our history notes one last time. Living a mission-possible life, in whatever our hands find to do, is an act of worship. Even if we feel we have little to offer in terms of money or talent, we are mission forward when we choose to use what we have to glorify God. In 1 Corinthians 3:9, Paul reminds us that "we are God's fellow workers." Whether paid or unpaid, recognized or overlooked, behind a desk or on a field, we are partakers of a divine nature.

I recently received a beautiful letter from a seventeen-year-old girl named Fiorella Siu. Fiorella lives in El Salvador, a country she noted is the smallest in Central America. Even before I continued to read the letter, that intentional detail reminded me of the story of Gideon in the Bible. God called Gideon a "valiant warrior" (Judges 6:12) and commanded him to rise up and save the nation of Israel. Gideon refused at first, offering what he felt was a legitimate excuse: "O Lord, how am I to save Israel? Behold, my family is the least in Manasseh, and I am the youngest in my father's house" (verse 15). I've learned that God can do much with our little. If we hold on to what we have, that's all we have. But if we give God even that which we consider insignificant, God will not only receive it but also multiply it.

Never overestimate what you can do by your own power, and never underestimate what God can do when you offer what you have and who you are fully to Him.

Fiorella knows what it's like to suffer—from developing symptoms that mirrored the signs of leukemia but were ultimately healed in her body, to witnessing firsthand her parents' financial devastation when she was ten years old and remembering what it was like to stand in a grocery store with only a dollar in her hand. These struggles didn't harden her spirit; they strengthened her dependence on God and shaped her heart to beat toward others. Knowing how it felt to be without, her parents always encouraged her to help others, to share food when someone is hungry, and to show God's love when someone feels lost or afraid.

Fiorella wrote,

I've always felt like I can't fit in with the youth of nowadays, but now my way of looking at things is different. I've always had this urge to evangelize and show God's love for others, but sometimes I feel like I'm not old enough or don't have enough money to make an impact in this world.

I've finally understood that my life is not always going to be about myself. God has chosen me to make a difference. What really matters is how I lived to help others and show His love through the small acts I can do.

As a family, we pray for God's blessing so that we can bless others. I no longer care about the material things or how successful I can be on earth but on the souls I impact by sharing God's love. The most important thing I can do is reflect Jesus's attributes so that other people can experience how important they are to God. When I realized that I wanted to reflect Jesus, my way of viewing things and interacting with others, even with my family, has changed. Now I'm more aware of how I speak and how I treat others. Now I'd rather care about what God thinks of me than what others will. I'd rather be criticized for being "weird" than disappoint God for trying to fit in with the crowd.

From now on, I want to put others' lives and needs above my own. I really want to be remembered as a symbol of God's love to others. I know that God will see my heart and desires and that He can use them to make miracles like he used the five loaves of bread and two fish of a little young man to feed thousands.

Fiorella, I have a pretty good feeling that God sees your heart, and He is so proud of you!

We may feel insignificant or unseen, or we may think our talents pale in comparison to what we see on social media, but when we offer God our willingness in everything we do, we position ourselves for miracles, for eternal impact, and for increasing a spiritual legacy no one can take away. When our lives are immersed in **avad**—like the lives of Miss Nancy, Daniel, and Fiorella—we breed opportunities to grow and to live out our missions.

Never overestimate what you can do by your own power, and never underestimate what God can do when you offer what you have and who you are fully to Him.

I believe that even if the little boy had only one loaf of bread and one fish, Jesus would have still performed the same miracle. It's not your stuff God wants or needs; it's your willingness to live your life, every part of it, for Him.

4

MISSION-POSSIBLE
SUPERPOWERS

The pursuit of God is not a
part-time, weekend exercise. . . .
It is a pursuit of passion.
—R. C. SPROUL

MY FATHER HAS DONE AND SAID MANY
things that have made me rethink my perspective,
shaped my worldview, and overall made me a better
man. I'll never forget what he did for me when I was
eight years old. Though it shocked me then, over the
years it has revolutionized my definition of passion.

At the time, my father had spent a few months
serving in the Philippines while Mom was at home
in Jacksonville, Florida, taking care of us five kids.
We missed him terribly. The day he arrived back in
the States was like Christmas, even without the spar-
kling lights and red-and-green overload. When we

saw Dad coming toward us in the airport, we bolted toward him. Each of us kids grabbed some part of him and hung on for dear life. None of us wanted to let go. It was a moving spectacle. Time stopped for us in that moment, but we couldn't stay at the airport forever. Dad drove us home that afternoon as we peppered him with questions while Mom held his hand. Our reunion revelry came to a halt when we noticed he pulled off the highway one exit before the one that led us home.

"Where are we going?" one of my siblings chimed from the back of the car.

"Just hang on," Dad replied with a wink. "You'll see when we get there." Mom just nodded and smiled. Looking back, I don't think she knew where we were going, but she trusted him. After leaving us kids to our imaginative devices trying to specu- late what fun-filled surprise awaited us, he pulled into a parking lot. I may not have recognized what roads we were on or what part of town we were in, but I sure recognized that huge yellow-and-blue sign shaped like a ripped ticket stub. In bold yellow let- ters, the word **Blockbuster** greeted the Tebow fam- ily. Remember that store? Go ahead—take a minute to tap into your memory of the greatest video store chain in the world. Can you feel the deep disap- pointment that would overwhelm your soul when on a Friday night the last copy of the new release you'd been dying to watch had just been snagged? Or maybe you relate better to getting grounded by your parents for racking up late fees because you were too lazy to return a video in the drop box. Or how about the simplest and most telling test of character: "Be kind, rewind." If reading those last three words put a smile on your face, congratulations. You are officially old-school.

Fun fact before I dive into why Dad stopped at Blockbuster. There's only one remaining Blockbuster in the world. At the twenty-year-old store in Bend, Oregon, you can still rent a movie on a clunky VHS cassette. You can also spend the night there with your closest friends and enjoy a movie marathon of your choice (and free pizza).[1]

Dad walked into Blockbuster and returned to the car holding a blue-and-yellow plastic bag that housed, we assumed, a movie rental. After listening to an animated barrage of "What did you get?" Dad calmly told us, "You'll see when we get home." Worst reply ever.

My sisters may have been hoping that Dad had rented **Clueless,** but that was unlikely. We assumed it wasn't **Die Hard: With a Vengeance** because of its R rating, but who knew? Because it wasn't like Dad to rent movies, especially after having been gone from us for so long, even our best guesses couldn't solve this mystery.

After we got home and gave Dad a chance to settle in, he called out for me and my two brothers to meet him in the family room. Anticipation twisted and turned its way in my stomach. I can't remember if he offered us some background about the movie before we watched it. He did set it up, however, with a moving speech that echoes in my ears today.

As Dad spoke to us, tears flooded his face. I don't remember exactly what he said verbatim, but he had our utmost attention. To the best of my memory, it went something like this: "I just want you to know how much I love you and how proud I am of you and how I believe in you. I know that all of you are ambitious and you want to accomplish things in your life. It's my job as your dad to give you an edge, to give you an advantage, so that you're not like every other person and so you remember that you are unique. In a moment, I'm going to hit play on this movie. And first I want you to watch it and really study it, especially the main character. Because, boys, if you love whatever it is that you do, like the man you're going to see in this movie, you will be different. You will be special."

He took a breath and continued: "Second, I want you to have passion like this man for whatever it is that you want to do. Third, I want you to be willing to sacrifice, because if you're willing to love what you do, be passionate about it, and be willing to sacrifice for whatever it is, you're going to be different. You're going to be contagious. You're going to be special, and people are going to want to be around you."

Then he pressed play on the VCR and sat down on the couch next to Mom. Obviously, I didn't know the man from the film he was referring to—Dad had just watched the film on the plane ride back home, by the way—but the main character's name was spoken in the first minute of the opening scene. That scene begins innocently enough with the droning melody of bagpipes serenading dreamy shots of rugged mountains and a misty sky, but it gives way to a young William Wallace witnessing the aftermath of a massacre. Yeah, I wasn't quite prepared for that. I'm talking, of course, about **Braveheart,** the epic historical-fiction account of the legendary Wallace, one of Scotland's historic national heroes. If you haven't seen it, watch it. I've probably watched that film a hundred times, and I even have a poster of it in my man cave.

Braveheart tells the story of a Scottish warrior who rallies his countrymen in the late 1200s against the brutal British monarch who rules Scotland. His quest for independence is partly fueled by the assault and murder of his wife at the hands of English soldiers. His mission is to lead his country to freedom so his people can live free from British tyranny. The road to freedom was paved with sacrifice and ultimately required Wallace to pay for it with his life. Deemed a traitor by the British government, he was hanged, drawn, and quartered.

You might be thinking, **An eight-year-old watching** Braveheart? I'll admit, it was a little intense. My mom was absolutely mortified. Aside from the fact that it features many gory battle scenes, there were a few instances that portrayed mild nudity. Like a good mother, she tried her best to cover our eyes during those parts. In Dad's defense, he watched the edited airplane version, so many of the scenes were a bit of a surprise to him too. Now, considering I was young when I watched the movie for the first time, I wasn't really prepared to process—from a psychological or spiritual perspective—all the complicated themes the film portrayed.

What did I think at the time? Well, while I was incredibly inspired, I admit some parts were baffling. I was traumatized that Robert the Bruce, a Scottish lord who promised Wallace his allegiance in uniting against the British, ended up betraying him. I couldn't figure out why Wallace wouldn't accept whatever he was offered to drink by the princess to mitigate the pain of being tortured. The biggest question I had was how a movie could be considered so amazing when the main character, in this case the courageous leader of a noble revolution, dies at the end.

But even with all those questions, I knew one thing: I wanted to live with fierce courage and passion as Wallace did.

As I got older and rewatched the film many times, I began to understand its underlying themes of conviction and perseverance. And I truly appreciated the wisdom Dad imparted to us through this film.

Passion Meets Purpose

That **Braveheart** viewing wasn't the only time my dad taught us the importance of passion for a cause. He'd repeat the same message over the years: when he'd drop me off for church events, sports practices, and games and when we'd toss the ball around in the yard. "Love what you do," he'd tell me. "Be passionate about it. It's so important that you go after what you really love to do and that matters."

I like to think of passion as a superpower.

Most superheroes have special abilities that help them withstand challenges and overcome obstacles. Those superpowers set them apart from mere mortals as well as their enemies. Take the most recognizable superhero, Superman. His core superpowers include flight, speed, strength, and X-ray vision. As familiar of a character as he is to most of us, he has some superhero characteristics that are not commonly known. For instance, he can clone himself. In one episode, he is depicted as being in two places at once to save Lois. He also has a super kiss. He smooched Lois so passionately one particular time that he wiped out her memory. She couldn't remember that Clark Kent and Superman were the same person. I guess the writers meant that to be sweet at the time, but it's a little creepy in hindsight.

When it comes to purpose and being mission minded, many of us are drawn to certain characteristics we believe top the grade scale. Like talent or skill or platform. And these characteristics can be quite effective. When we listen to a skilled speaker or musician, it's easy to determine how their talents contribute to the mission they are pursuing. When you have a far-reaching audience, you have more power and opportunity to influence the masses. Certainly, those characteristics we admire are valuable. But there are characteristics of being mission driven that we all have that don't necessarily stem from obvious sources. I believe one of the most paramount and accessible requirements of living a mission-possible life is passion.

Passion today has everything to do with an intense desire; the word is typically used when describing sex or romance. We think we see it when a man pursues a woman (or the reverse can be true as well). He is so in love with her that he does everything in his power to win her heart. He writes her schmaltzy love songs. He buys her elaborate gifts. He is relentless in his pursuit. Passion, in the form of a half-naked ripped guy clutching what looks like a damsel in distress, is depicted on the cover of most romance novels. There's a reason this is one of the most popular genres of books. But those illustrations of passion are a far cry from the word's true meaning. The word has been diluted over time.

Passion is deeper than feeling excited or being hyped up. It's got more layers than a fickle emotion. It's ingrained deep in your soul. The word **passion** was first introduced in the twelfth century. It comes from the Latin root word **pati,** which means "to suffer." I don't know anyone who would pick the word **suffer** as a synonym for **passion.** The Latin word for passion was first used to describe the death of Jesus. Jesus's arrest, subsequent torture, and death by crucifixion are the events sometimes referred to as Passion narratives. So, it turns out that the true story of passion is a story about suffering.

If you want to have the passion that fuels a mission-possible life, do something that you are willing to suffer for. This suffering is not a form of self-masochism. It's not about torturing yourself for a greater cause. It's about being willing to stick it out and fight for what you believe in when the glitz and glamour vanish and no one is watching.

> **It turns out that the true story of passion is a story about suffering.**

While Chad Hymas was building his elk farm in Utah, he broke his neck in a freak accident that rendered him a paraplegic at twenty-seven years old. As he recovered from his injury and reintroduced his new body to his old life, he wanted to achieve a goal most would believe would be impossible. He refused to allow his paralysis to limit his experiences, so he began to build bigger expectations for himself.

Two years later, in 2003, he logged 513 miles

in 104 hours over 11 days by pushing himself in a three-wheeled bike from downtown Salt Lake City, Utah, to Las Vegas, Nevada. It's roughly a 6.5-hour car ride. I read Chad's story in the book **Aspire: Discovering Your Purpose Through the Power of Words,** written by Kevin Hall, who accompanied Chad on part of his adventure. Kevin describes the celebratory onset of the journey—how the route was paved with excitement and visible support. There were police escorts, large cheering crowds, and cameras from many different media outlets recording this remarkable and inspirational journey.

But Kevin also shows the darker part of Chad's journey: "It wouldn't be until later, when the TV lights and police escorts were long gone, when there was no one on the curb to applaud and encourage, when the road turned upward, when his arms ached, when he was tired and hungry, that it would get difficult."[2] Even when the excitement faded, Chad was willing to suffer for his passion. He saw the other side of being weary. Chad easily could have decided to give up after such a severe injury, but he had a passion to make a difference through his suffering and beyond his pain.

When you get tired, true passion is what will see you through. When no one is around to help boost your confidence, passion will help you take the next step. When you get stuck or hit a wall, passion will give you momentum to recover and press forward. In your desire to live armed with purpose, find out where your passions lie. What are you willing to sacrifice for? What are you willing to pursue or stand up or fight for in the face of challenge and adversity?

The passion of William Wallace as portrayed in **Braveheart** was evident throughout much of the movie. His desire to avenge his wife's death and his mission to vanquish the English rule is undergirded by a passion—not just a powerful feeling, but an unwavering belief in something he was willing to suffer for. As an underdog, not having come from Scottish royalty and wielding no real authority, he manages to unite an army of Scots to fight with him for their freedom. Even if you haven't seen the movie, you might have watched the scene where Wallace, smeared with blue-and-white war paint, gallops on a horse in front of a motley crew of Scottish rebels. Wallace is primed to fight, but the makeshift soldiers are not so convinced fighting this battle will result in any good, let alone their independence. In a stirring speech, he rallies the army of unambitious Scots to march forward and fight instead of running home and dying a coward's death.

Wallace says, "Aye, fight and you may die. Run and you'll live—at least a while. And dying in your beds, many years from now, would you be willin' to trade all the days, from this day to that, for one chance, just one chance, to come back here and tell our enemies that they may take our lives, but they'll never take our freedom!"[3]

His passion-fueled mission inspired the men to

fight, and ultimately, years later, after Wallace was executed as a traitor by the British government, the Scots gained their independence.

> **Each person's journey is unique. Don't look to your best friend or colleague to find what moves your spirit and what you choose to fight for. You are one of one.**

If you already know where your passion lies, you probably have at least a glimpse of what a mission-possible life looks like for you. If that's true, awesome! If anything I've said has made you want to find your passion, here are some prompts to help recalibrate your direction:

1. **What do you enjoy doing?** What do you look forward to doing that fires you up and builds within you an unshakable enthusiasm? Volunteering at a local animal shelter? Helping people? Spending time with the elderly? Working on a committee to target problems in your community and figuring out solutions to fix them?

2. **Who do you want to help the most?** This question ties into the one above and narrows

your focus. Is your heart moved with compassion toward people with learning disabilities? Do you champion the cause of the underprivileged in this country or abroad? Who makes your heart bleed or cry or melt or tremble?

3. What problem do you want to help solve? Do you care about people having clean water? Would you prefer to work with inmates and tackle prison reform? Are you drawn to providing nutrition to children who live in food-insecure homes? What value do you offer?

4. Are there any themes in what you read, listen to, talk about, and research? Think about all you do in a day, the shows you watch, the podcasts you enjoy, and your Googling habits. Are there any recurring concepts?

When you're thick in the process of discovering your passion, remind yourself that each person's journey is unique. Don't look to your best friend or colleague to find what moves your spirit and what you choose to fight for. You are one of one. We were not created to be replicas of anyone else. I love this quote that's been attributed to Albert Einstein: "Everybody is a genius. But if you judge a fish by its ability to climb a tree, it will live its whole life believing that it is stupid." You don't need to be passionate

about something or someone merely because some-
one else is. Find the passion that beats to the rhythm
of your own heart.

Find and Use Your Edge

There's something about having to do more with less
growing up that developed in me an inner drive, or
what I like to call an edge. My parents didn't have
a lot of money when they were raising us kids. And
although we weren't endowed with designer clothes
or fancy vacations, Mom and Dad instilled in us a
work ethic I nurture to this day, as well as a drive
that feeds my desire to pursue my dreams and strive
to be the best at them. This didn't come from an up-
bringing that cultivated entitlement; it was birthed
in learning the value of a dollar and the blessing of
hard work.

"Anyone want a Gatorade?" I can't tell you how
many times I heard those words playing sports as
a kid. Every little hand around me would shoot up
except mine. "No thanks. I've got water," I'd say. It
wasn't that I didn't like Gatorade. Of course I did!
But I also knew that it was a lot more expensive
than good ol' H_2O (and not the bottled kind—the
kind that gushed from a tap and was poured into
a reusable bottle). Mom and Dad were missionar-
ies. Living on a limited income taught them to be

frugal, and that meant Gatorade wasn't on our grocery list. It also meant that going out to lunch after church on Sundays wasn't a recurring event and that the only time we'd be able to enjoy a snow cone after games was when our team would win, because then the cones were free.

My parents' intentional financial practices also gave us kids room to contribute to our family. Mom and Dad were definitely equal-opportunity employers. Growing up on a farm, we had all the fruits and vegetables we wanted and then some. We ate and sold what we helped grow. Sell what you sow, right?

When I was in Little League, every now and then in between games and practices, I'd grab whatever basket of fresh vegetables Mom or Dad had brought that day and walk around the stands selling what I could. This may have impressed the parents a bit, but the kids got quite a kick out of it. They'd lavish me with ridicule, doing their best to try to make me look and feel stupid. Whatever. I never let their sneers or jabs bother me. I was a confident kid and able to pull off selling cucumbers, squash, and zucchini as if it were something any cool kid would do.

I've never gotten a trophy for gardening, but from years of picking the fruits of our labor on our farm, I discovered a few things. The most practical lesson I learned was to wear gloves and long sleeves, as some fruits and vegetables are more aggressive in nature than others. Take okra, for instance. This slimy fruit is covered in tiny spines that can easily prick and itch your skin. Pitching with okra hands was not fun, so I learned quickly to protect my skin while peddling the Tebows' goods.

As I learned to take care of my hands, my parents also taught me how to take care of all the other stuff the good Lord had given me. In the context of Little League, this meant my bat. I remember the first new one my parents ever gave me. It was Redline. And the first time I used it, I hit a home run. The gravity of the purchase wasn't lost on me. Many teammates were going through two or three bats a season. I was the kid who always had to borrow a bat or use the team's equipment. Having my own bat and one that had never been used before filled me with a great sense of pride. I handled the athletic instrument with care when it wasn't swinging in my hands, resisting the urge to chuck it on the ground in frustration. I knew how hard my parents had worked to honor me with my own bat, and I didn't want to take it for granted. I used that bat for years—the same one, every game, every practice.

Watching my parents stretch a dollar and hustling as many cucumbers as I could impressed upon me the truth that even the most expensive glove or the best cleats weren't going to magically make me faster or stronger. But an edge would. Dad may not have been able to get me the latest Jordans, but he'd spray-paint the driveway so I could run drills. He may not have been able to afford to buy me a gym membership or a Bowflex, but he took the time to weld together whatever weights he could find so I could get in a good workout. He also built my brothers and me a batting cage made out of wood and fishing nets and would throw to us for hours and hours when he wasn't abroad. I'll never forget the day football face masks went on sale at a local sporting goods store. All the good athletes had one, except me. They were too expensive. Mom was so excited when she found one we could afford, except it was the wrong color. That afternoon, Mom and I spent time together, kneeling over a floor of newspapers we had put down to spray-paint my helmet the correct color of our team. It felt amazing to finally have a face mask like the other kids. Even so, my confidence came not from the painted mask but from the edge my parents instilled in me as we made it.

My parents didn't need a ton of money to show their kids how to hustle and work hard. Their gifts to us didn't require a penny and came in the form of discipline, drive, and ingenuity. I chose not to perceive what they couldn't give me as a disadvantage but rather as an opportunity to strengthen my natural abilities, putting in longer hours, training harder, and stepping it up when it stopped feeling fun. If I ever have children one day, I pray I can give them that same loving support I received and help shape for them an edge that material things cannot provide.

I'm sure you've heard the word **edge** used in different platforms. It's actually the title of one of my favorite books, one I borrowed from my strength coach in college. Thanks for loaning it to me, Coach. I promise I'll give it back to you one day!

An edge might mean an advantage that makes you stand apart from your competitors, or a unique trait that makes you stronger, faster, smarter, or, as I've heard it once said, the line that you cross to feel alive. **Edge** can be defined as "an improved position or advantage." I consider edge to be an intestinal fortitude that stems from our passion, grows from our experiences (positive or negative), and revs up in the face of opposition.

I used my family's financial situation to find my edge. My family couldn't afford the kind of gear most kids had, but that lack forged in me a mental determination to be the best. Every season of every sport, I seemed to start with a deficit. You could hear our parents' car, the weary van with the hole in the floor, twenty-two miles away. It definitely wasn't helping the community go green. I'd show up on the field with cleats that were torn up because I'd had them for two years or that were too big because Mom and Dad wanted me to have them for two years. The kids would make fun of me at the start of each season, but I used that mockery to stir in me a passion to put in the work—extra work. I may not have had a gym membership, but I had a hard-work membership. My mentality, even as a kid, was, "I may not be wearing the most expensive cleats, but I'm going to be the fastest and the strongest member on this team."

I truly believe that if I'd had the financial advantages other kids had, it would have been a detriment to me. I wouldn't have gained the edge that I nurtured as I got older and even after I could afford the fancy cleats. In a way, this fortitude looked like a chip—no, a boulder—on my shoulder. And I used it to my advantage. I knew how hard my parents worked, and I believed in them so much I wanted to honor that by pushing my limits physically, which was a catalyst in strengthening my mental edge. I love what Coach Urban Meyer has said: "Edge is where average stops and elite begins."[4] Find your edge and use it. It'll take you beyond what you imagine are your limits.

Having an edge doesn't mean you'll meet all your goals and accomplish every single thing you've set out to achieve, but it gives you the best chance at being different. As Dad said, we don't have to be like everyone else. We can set ourselves apart in a good way. We can do it our way, equipped and empowered not by human strength or skill but by the Spirit of God living within us. You may not strive to be an athlete, but you can have an edge because God has called you to be different. Your perfect is yours alone. Take that into account. When society tells you that you have to be this or wear that or say this or do that, you can have the confidence from your experience to withstand that pressure and pursue your mission and live life your way.

The Edge That Can Change a Life

What's your superhero edge? Before you start thinking of what you are not or what you don't have, think of what you've gained from your experiences. What have you overcome? What do you know more of now because of what you went through yesterday? Maybe you know what it's like to fight for something—your family, your health, sobriety—and be victorious against the odds. However grueling the experience, you've come out emotionally and mentally stronger. You know you can grit your teeth, fight, and win. That intentional fortitude, as sucky as the experience it was pulled from was, is your edge. Maybe it's your patience or knowledge. Maybe homeschooling four children doesn't strip you to tears. Maybe you have what it takes to invest your time and knowledge in them and help create contributing members of our society, boys and girls who can one day rule the world. Whatever your edge, use it to live mission forward.

My friend Mario loves people. He has made it his mission to promote friendship and kindness. Doing that is especially important to him because he knows what it's like to be bullied by classmates and strangers. This funny, loving, easygoing superhero is a blast' to be around. Mario is confident in his value as an amazing human being, which makes it hard for him to accept how cruel and mean people can be to him.

Mario was born two months premature in the back of an ambulance bay of a small community hospital. He didn't have a pulse and required seven minutes of CPR in the ambulance to revive him. Once he was stable enough, baby Mario was rushed into the emergency room. He was diagnosed with two rare illnesses: sacral agenesis, which is the abnormal development of the spine and major organs, and Goldenhar syndrome, which includes deformities of the eyes, ears, and spine. Although Mario can't walk on his feet, he's learned to walk on his hands and is pretty sick at doing handstands. His medical issues at birth were so complicated a doctor in the emergency room said that if he had delivered Mario, he would not have revived him as the paramedic in the ambulance had.

Mario was in the hospital for much of the first three years of his life. His biological mother was homeless and couldn't care for him. His father was in prison in another country. Mario was placed in the foster care system, and when he was about five years old, he was adopted by a wonderful woman named Donna Claussen and her husband, Tom. Of all the complex challenges Mario has overcome, the hardest thing he has endured is the bullying. He is regularly stared at, pointed at, called names, teased about his appearance, and chased by both kids and adults. One morning he told Donna that he wanted to put an end to bullies. She was doubtful that anything could be done.

In the face of the impossible, Mario chose to fight for kindness. After talking about his mission with his adoptive mother, that day they began his kindness campaign called Stand with Mario. Mario started making bracelets and giving them to kids who have been bullied. The idea was that whenever they felt sad or lonely, they could look at the bracelet and be reminded that they aren't alone. He added more products to his line, including shirts, hats, cups, cookies, and Christmas cards. All the proceeds are donated to help purchase buddy benches at schools across the country. Placed in a schoolyard, a buddy bench is a safe place for a child to make a new friend. A school who has acquired a buddy bench holds an assembly, often with Mario as the guest speaker, in which the purpose of the bench is explained. If a child is new to the school, lonely, being picked on, alienated, or just needs a new friend, he or she simply sits on the bench. When the other kids see the person sitting there, they are encouraged to invite him or her to play or be their friend.

A mission-possible life isn't constructed from a cocktail of privilege, a diploma from a top-tier institution, high-end gear, or social status; it is rooted in what God has made each one of us to be.

Mario has turned the pain he has endured from being treated unkindly into a blessing for others. This is his edge, his superpower. God has used him to bless so many lives. He's helped remind people how special they are and influenced those around him to treat other people who may not look or act like them with kindness and respect.

A mission-possible life isn't constructed from a cocktail of privilege, a diploma from a top-tier institution, high-end gear, or social status; it is rooted in what God has made each one of us to be. We might not pave the way to freedom from tyranny, but armed with passion and edge, we can definitely change a life. Like passion, an edge is contagious. People will notice and be inspired by it. This is mission-possible living! You live with passion and edge not so you can have an easy and comfortable life in the limelight but so you can be an encouragement to others on their journey.

I have an edge because I believe in God and because He has been and will be faithful. The more you fall in love with Jesus, and the more you understand the edge He gives you, the more you are willing to go out on a limb and even suffer for something you believe in. Ultimately, for each believer, that sacrifice, that passion, is what it means to win the race of faith.

5

PURPOSE IN THE PRESENT

The great doesn't happen through impulse alone, and is a succession of little things that are brought together.
—Vincent van Gogh

I'LL NEVER FORGET THE FIRST TIME the idea of hosting proms for kids with special needs, which has come to be known as Night to Shine, came about. I was talking to our director of the foundation at the time about our upcoming fifth anniversary.

He mentioned he knew of two churches in the country who were hosting special dances for people with developmental disabilities. "Since you and the foundation love people with special needs, would you want to do something like that to celebrate our five-year anniversary?"

"Absolutely!"

"Awesome! So right here in Jacksonville?"

I didn't have to think twice. "Everywhere. I'd like to host these events all around the world!"

He looked at me like I had sprouted four heads. "No, seriously."

"I **am** serious." From what I'd heard about what these dances had looked like, plus what I'd seen over the years of how people with special needs are treated in countries where they are discounted and literally discarded, I knew I wanted to take this celebration abroad. I had big dreams in that moment (not that I knew how to execute them or even where to start). The only thing I did know was that God loves each and every one of us.

I didn't want to just host a cool event; I wanted to offer an experience guests would never forget. But it wouldn't be about the glitz and glamour of an amazing night of dancing and fun. That stuff is good and makes people smile, but it's the love of God that changes hearts and souls. And in my mind, that's what the event was about. Not a party, but a showering of God's love.

As we started quickly moving toward making this event a reality, many people around us had questions, even a few folks who were really close to our team. I'll be the first to admit that the concerns behind the questions were sincere. I totally get why they were being asked. Questioning helps us solve problems and gather knowledge. And as this was the first time we were doing something like this, I may not have had the best answers to the questions, though I couldn't shake the feeling that we needed to passionately pursue this dream.

But in this instance, all these questions seemed to distract and detract from the vision. It seemed as if some people were trying to prompt doubt instead of promote possibility—looking for a way out instead of a way in. Although I knew we needed careful thought and planning, I wasn't going to toss the idea on a back burner just because we didn't have a fifty-page plan on how we were going to execute this mission.

I knew I had to listen to the pull of my heart, and I believed that this idea was aligned with Scripture. The more conversations our team had about it and the more pushback we faced, the more my faith grew and the more I knew that having this event felt right. That said, I didn't know exactly how or if it would work, but I just wanted to help people feel loved, and this was a channel to help make that happen. See, my mission was never to put on Night to Shine. Now, I love it and it's absolutely my favorite night of the year, but my mission was, and continues to be, loving and celebrating and caring for those whom God loves and celebrates and cares for. And step by step, even in the face of resistance, the clearer it seemed that Night to Shine was one way to accomplish this mission.

Have you ever avoided doing something because you didn't have all the answers? Has your idea ever fallen flat because you got hung up on having every-thing figured out? You've heard of paralysis by analy-sis, right? The phrase might be a cliché, but it likely became one because it's true.

We want to do the right thing. We want to pursue our missions. But our passion can start to fade if God doesn't show up in our dreams with a step-by-step blueprint for **how** and **where** and **why** everything is going to pan out. Why is it that when we don't have **all** the information, we tend to do nothing?

Time waits for no one. Having no compassion or empathy, it marches on. A few months pass, a year or more, and hardly anything has changed. We still haven't made much movement in any direction.

Pursue the <u>What,</u> and God Will Take Care of the <u>Why</u> and <u>How</u>

I know what it's like to pray and ask for God's guid-ance or approval in certain decisions and not audibly hear a response. I've experienced many challenges in my life that made me feel completely stuck. I've prayed and asked the Lord to show me the answer. I sought wise counsel. I talked to pastors. But I still felt stuck. Not hearing specific guidance or direction doesn't mean that God isn't leading me, nor does it mean He is not with me.

Part of walking by faith and not by sight (see 2 Corinthians 5:7) is that sometimes we just don't know what God wants us to do. We may believe we have a sense of where He is leading us, but often He doesn't leak the details.

One common thread I see in the Bible is God handing out assignments in which He reveals the **what** (and sometimes not too much of that) and very little of the **how** and **why.** It seems like He's always on a mission to give us opportunities to depend on Him rather than on external resources or our own devices.

You might remember the story of Noah and the ark (see Genesis 6:13–7:24). When he was just over five hundred years old, he became a dad. During the period Noah was working a twelve-hour shift and changing diapers, God had an unusual mission for him. Not only was this mission something that hadn't been done before, but it was also going to take an indecorous amount of time during which its construction would seem as pointless as pushing an elevator button multiple times just in case it didn't get the message the first time.

"There's going to be a flood, so build an ark so I can save you and your family," God told Noah and proceeded to give him detailed instructions regarding its construction, such as the dimensions and the building materials needed. As the dumbstruck man tried to regain his composure, God added, "Oh, and bring two of every living thing with you so the animal kingdom can continue to procreate."

Here's the kicker. There is no mention of **falling**

rain in the Bible before the flood. The earth, according to some scholars, may have been watered by only a mist. Others believe the amount of water in the ground was sufficient to hydrate the earth's vegetation or that humans may have created a type of irrigation system. In any case, it's likely the inhabitants of the earth didn't ever need to check a weather app to see if they should bring their umbrella or cancel a pool party. Nobody could have anticipated a **violent** rainstorm, let alone a flood. They were in for quite a surprise.

It could have taken Noah close to a hundred years to build this massive ship. A hundred years! I waited a long time to meet the right woman, but I don't know if I could have waited another seventy or eighty years. Can you imagine building a house that takes that long? I've never done construction, but I know what it feels like to be sacked by a defensive end. It's not fun. I can imagine that building a ship that measured around half the length and a quarter of the height of the largest cruise ship in the world, the **Symphony of the Seas,** was nothing short of backbreaking labor.

Noah must have been exhausted after measuring twice, cutting once, and hammering all day. Picture with me what it must have felt like to be him. Noah takes a seat and settles on the gopher-wood floor. He smiles, beaming proud at its smooth surface. Not a bad sanding job for a first-timer. Biting into his peanut-butter-and-jelly sandwich, he tries to ignore his bickering coworkers: his three sons, who can't agree on anything, including how to manage construction tasks among them. It is only day thirty, and the framework built barely resembles the skeleton of a massive ship. But it is something that wasn't there thirty days ago.

Noah's day will be over soon, and while he is looking forward to his wife's gentle hands kneading his knotted back muscles, he is also dreading the sarcastic jabs and whispers of his neighbors. People are starting to talk. It's hard to miss his massive building project in the middle of the neighborhood.

"An ark? He's got nothing better to do? Why doesn't he get a job?"

"God spoke to him? Really? What makes him so special?"

"I bet you five goats he's having a midlife crisis."

Noah is careful not to advertise his doubts out loud. And although he doesn't totally agree with others' opinions of this ark, he can't ignore that dull gnawing in his spirit: **Is this some sort of sick joke or twisted test? How much longer can I keep up this grueling pace? Any more calluses and blisters and my beautiful wife will refuse to hold my hand. Will rain really come? This doesn't make sense. None of it does!**

While the questions surface as Noah chews and contemplates his mission, he sighs. What else is he going to do? And flicking off the crumbs stuck on his beard, the man picks up his hammer and keeps going. **Bam, bam, bam!**

One day, shortly after turning six hundred years old (see 7:6), Noah notices the sky mysteriously darken well before sunset. Lightning cracks in the distance. And out of nowhere, a blanket of angry clouds begins to shroud every inch of daylight, the overture to a downpour of rain pelting the ground. Noah and his family take cover in the ark. As rolling thunder shakes the ship, Noah remembers what God told him: "After seven more days, I will send rain on the earth for forty days and forty nights" (verse 4). Almost a century has passed since Noah had listened without interruption to God's mission command.

What can we learn from this man who had stayed faithful, on course, even in the face of many questions and doubts?

It's not about knowing every detail or having an answer for every question; it's about accepting the mission God has prompted in your heart and following it, one step at a time. It's about being obedient and being open to where He is leading. If He says to stay, you stay. If He says to go, you go. If His leading is for you to homeschool your kids, do it. If it's to go back to school, start filling out the application. If it's to create support in your neighborhood, start on your block.

It's not about knowing every detail or having an answer for every question; it's about accepting the mission God has prompted in your heart and following it, one step at a time.

You move forward in your mission even if you make a mistake or take a wrong turn. Let's park here for a sec. Mission-possible living is not about perfection; it's about a person, and that person is Jesus. The same principle applies to the Christian life. Walking by faith isn't about never messing up; it's about acknowledging that we are made righteous because we've placed our trust in Jesus. If you find yourself off track because you made the wrong decision or stumbled along the way, don't focus on pursuing perfection. There will never be a day in which we make perfect choices, have the perfect thoughts, and make all the right moves. I'm so glad imperfections don't disqualify us from finishing the race.

The only thing that keeps us from moving mission forward is ourselves. We are responsible for keeping it moving, even if it's taking us longer than expected, even when our friends think we're crazy, and even if others question our motives. When you don't know what to do, depend on God. You don't need it all figured out. You just need Him to know it. And He does it. The Bible tells us, "Oh, the depth of the riches, both of the wisdom and knowledge of God! How unsearchable are His judgments and unfathomable His ways! For who has known the mind of the LORD, or who became His counselor?" (Romans 11:33–34). We can't figure God out. And you know what? I don't want to serve a God I can figure out. If we could, we'd hang right on His level, and if we did that, we wouldn't need Him at all. God has the details figured out. He knows the twists and turns that are coming, as well as the opportunities and provision. Rest in this and find peace that His knowledge is greater than ours.

In your pursuit of a mission-possible life, the questions will come. Don't treat them as a stop sign. It's an organic component of trusting God when you are stretched out of your comfort zone. Feel the questions, but just don't allow doubt to supersede action. Don't let the questions render you immobile.

The key is to start where you are. Be faithful in what God is telling you to do. Do your part, pray and keep praying, and let God do His work. But do something today. What can you do, starting now, to begin to live a mission-possible life?

Start Small

Zechariah 4:10 gives a much-needed reminder of the potential of something we may think is too

insignificant: "Do not despise these small beginnings, for the LORD rejoices to see the work
begin" (NLT).

You know where a mission-possible life begins?
With an idea. With one thought that swirls in the
mind that is not fully vetted. It's small. It's as insignificant as a single seed, yet it contains potential.
An idea might come when you're faced with a need
that's not being met. A movie or a TED Talk may
push it into your consciousness. You wake up from a
dream and it may pop into your head. This one tiny
idea is not developed or calculated, but for some
reason it's been deposited on the inside of you. This
is what it can seem like when God is encouraging
you to move in a certain direction. One thought can
lead to places we've never imagined or can propel
another idea that can link to the first and create an
even bigger collusion.

Not only can great things come from the spark of
an idea, but they can also be created by one person,
one need, one problem, one issue. The foundation
exists and is changing lives all over the world because of Sherwin, a boy with special needs whom I
had met on a mission trip to the Philippines when I
was teenager. That one encounter planted an idea in
my head and a hope in my heart that are still growing and expanding to this day.

Your idea may come after an encounter with a person or after observing a need that you can fill. Don't
dismiss those thoughts. Don't brush off something

that seems small. Even what's hidden to the naked eye, such as the atom or the molecules in a vaccine, can wield more power than we can imagine. It can change the world or even save a life.

If you're mowing the lawn, taking a walk, or playing in the backyard and you see a butterfly gliding through the air, what do you do? If you're like most people, you gasp in awe. You pause whatever it is you're doing and watch this winged creature float with its coat of beautiful colors. You probably whip out your phone to snap a pic of its wonder. Butterflies are graceful and majestic. They have the power to stop people in their tracks with their gorgeousness.

But butterflies have a mortal enemy: rain. An average monarch butterfly, at five hundred milligrams, weighs about seven times as much as a large raindrop, a mass of roughly seventy milligrams.[1] One drop of water on a butterfly is like a person being pummeled by the mass of two bowling bowls in the form of water balloons. You can imagine the damage a raindrop can do to the paper-thin wings of a butterfly. Most of these winged creatures will sit out a rainstorm, for obvious reasons. But they have an internal fortitude, an armor within their wings, to keep them from being destroyed.[2] When a raindrop hits the surface of a butterfly, it ripples and spreads across the surface. A nanoscale wax layer on the butterfly's wings repels the water while microbumps act like needles and pop each smaller drop of water. This powerful combination reduces the amount of time and force the droplet has with the surface, which consequently lowers the effect it has on the butterfly.

Butterflies have power to do more than merely captivate our attention with their beauty. These tiny creatures contain optimized designs, only visible using a high-speed camera that can capture thousands of frames per second, that can be used to help solve challenges in the human world. Mimicking designs in nature for human purposes is known as biomimicry. Previous water-repellent products such as Gore-Tex, raincoats, and waterproof paint were created based on the design of the lotus leaf. Findings from the latest study on butterflies' wings could lead to more innovation.

The flitter of color out of nowhere that captured your attention? There is more to it than you even know. Be curious about and investigate the idea that appears before you, believing that God can use something small to do something great.

You might not realize the potential you have to live mission forward. You may not recognize the possibility that God can use you—yes, you!—to make a positive difference in the life of one or many. Don't dismiss an idea or a prompting that wells in your soul. Pay attention to it, and do something with it.

Research your options.

Talk to people who have done similar things.

Make a to-do list.

Read books and listen to podcasts.

Pray and fast.

Remain open to opportunities that lead you in the direction you'd like to go.

Write down things you feel God may be speaking to you about.

Start small. Don't obsess about changing the world. Start by changing one person. Maybe that's yourself. Maybe it means taking better care of your health so you can spend quality time playing with your children. Maybe it's helping an overwhelmed single parent by watching her children for the day or cleaning her house. Maybe it's volunteering in your community or helping out once a week at a local soup kitchen or nursing home. Use what moves you, what God has put inside your heart, and take one step forward in mission-possible living.

When I Knew This Was It

When the team and I began discussing Night to Shine in 2014, we worked tirelessly for the next four or five months to build a game plan for something that we had never done before. There were so many moving parts that we didn't fully have the experience of arranging: **How do we brand this the right way? What kind of rules do we need to set in place for our guests and volunteers? What would the red carpet look like? What are appropriate and doable entertainment options? How do we make**

**the event accessible to all types of special needs
and not compromise anyone's health? How much
of a budget do we plan for? How do we partner
with churches?** One of the biggest questions we had
was what to name the event.

Some options were Evening of Joy, A Night to
Remember, Shine Bright, and Night of Hope.
Although they weren't the worst ideas, I thought we
could do a better job of creating a name that matched
the brightness of the lives we would be celebrating.
I could visualize Sherwin, the boy I had met on a
mission trip to the Philippines when I was a teen-
ager, who had inspired me to create our foundation
and its mission statement. I pictured him leaning
on his escort while walking down a red carpet and
literally shining—shining with joy and shining from
the lights that flashed from cameras as they photo-
graphed him and other people with special needs. I
wanted these precious people to know their worth
and for the world to see it as well.

I wanted them to experience a fun night in which
they would be able to sense the glory of God shine
on them, because that's how special they are. Believe
it or not, coming up with and deciding on a name
was probably one of the most challenging parts of
this process. I may have been fastidious in my ap-
proach, probably to the point of irritating my team,
but the name had to be right. It said it all. Yes, it
was just one part of the entire movement, but what-
ever we would decide to call it would communicate

the mission. We finally landed on Night to Shine. The name encapsulated everything the evening was about. And in the next few months, we asked, researched, and answered heaps of questions that we compiled in a twenty-one-page book summarizing the what, why, and how of Night to Shine. We have added to the resource every year, and it's now more than seventy-five pages.

I'll never forget the moment I knew this event is what we were supposed to do. It was the Friday night before Valentine's Day 2015. We had partnered with forty-three churches in twenty-six states and three countries around the world to provide an unforgettable prom-night experience centered on God's love. I wish I were able to attend every prom we host, but because I can't clone myself, I can't. I do spend the week leading up to Night to Shine visiting churches all over the world to pray with teams, encourage churches, and show my love to would-be guests and volunteers. I also show up to as many undisclosed locations as I can the night of the event. I don't sleep much during that week, and it's the best kind of tired I know.

The first year we launched Night to Shine, I was accompanied by a team of people, including a donor family and some of the foundation's team members. The first church on our itinerary was the First Christian Church in North Carolina. All the planning, decision making, last-minute arrangements, and changing and making more changes led up to this moment. Butterflies exploded in my stomach. I was both nervous and excited. I felt the same palpable energy I have felt right before playing in a national championship.

Rather than pulling up to the front of the church, I went to the side parking lot to keep the spotlight on all the wonderful guests of honor. Enjoying privately what was happening publicly was most important to me. I got out of the car and watched the beginning of the evening unfold. A long red carpet led from the curb to the front door of the church. On the sidelines, enthusiastic volunteers stood shoulder to shoulder, cheering for each guest as cameras flashed. I watched the first guest—his arm draped around his escort, his parent or guardian or a volunteer from the host church—take his place. Decked out in a tux that looked too big for him, he flashed a smile and strutted down the red carpet with a confident swagger. I took a few steps closer, fifty feet away from the spectacle, and watched the next guest do the same. She was shier than the first, and I could tell she wasn't sure how to process the lavish attention. Her hands trembled as she grabbed hold of her escort, eyes wide at the people cheering for her. Walking with careful steps, she made it to the end of the red carpet, her face aglow with pride.

I paused thirty feet away, my eyes fixed on the long line of guests waiting for their turn to enter the prom, and then continued forward. My heart was overcome in that moment. This was it. This was part of my mission. This was the love of God in action. This was what it looks like to be embraced, accepted, and loved in the presence of His glory. It was hard to hold back the tears. I don't know how to best describe this in words, but as I crept closer to the crowd gathered at the beginning of the red carpet, it felt like I was swept up in a force field of God's protection. It was like a barrier that surrounded the event and specifically each guest that was created for a purpose and loved without measure by the Creator. Even though the journey to this night had been littered with criticism, doubt, and scrutiny, God's hand had guided it all along.

> **This was it. This was part of my mission. This was the love of God in action. This was what it looks like to be embraced, accepted, and loved in the presence of His glory.**

As I got closer to the crowd surrounding the red carpet, I said hello to some people, shook a couple of hands, and cheered for a few more guests. Then I noticed a girl about to make her way down the red carpet. I asked if I could escort her, and she said yes. I was already excited, but this girl spilled even more joy over into my heart. Being able to escort her down the red carpet reminded me of the love and joy that God brings to every king and queen all over the world.

Some of these young adults will never get the chance to participate in their high school prom or homecoming or even walk down an aisle to get married. As a matter of fact, during one of the last events I attended that evening, I was stopped by a mom who said exactly that about her daughter with special needs: "My daughter will never get married. She will never have a baby. But tonight she felt like a princess."

When I got into the car late that night to go back home, I couldn't stop crying. It wasn't because it was a fun night or a cool prom; it was because the world came together to celebrate part of God's creation that isn't celebrated, loved, or walked down a red carpet as often as it should be. All of our efforts were worth it just to hear that mom tell me how her daughter felt. The incredible feeling I had was better than the way I felt after even some of my biggest victories on the field. Funny, it wasn't even my idea. It was just my dream to take it around the world.

We did something good that night, and I wanted to do more of it.

I'm so glad we didn't turn back before we had all the answers. We would've missed out on so much goodness and joy and hope.

You don't know what God has in store for you when you step out and walk by faith. One idea or one thought that propels you into action, such as dropping off a Bible to someone in need or lavishing love and joy onto people who are normally looked at as though they don't belong, can change the course of their days, and even their lives. One step forward in a mission-possible life can unveil to you the glory of God you may never have experienced before.

It's my honor to share a letter that was written to our foundation from Jeneil, a volunteer at Night to Shine. Jeneil has a daughter, Rhema, who at the time of this writing is fourteen. At age two, Rhema was diagnosed with autism, apraxia, and a rare and stubborn seizure disorder. These things robbed her of her speech. A neurologist informed Jeneil that Rhema most likely suffered from an inability to comprehend language, also known as word deafness. "I thought it was all a cruel cosmic joke," Jeneil said. "My child named 'word' could not speak or understand a word."

When the opportunity to volunteer for Night to Shine arose, Jeneil couldn't wait to be part of the event. She signed up to be a buddy, which meant her job was to accompany a guest and ensure he or she had a great time. Confidentiality is very important to us at the foundation, particularly at these events. To protect the privacy of our guests, we always ask volunteers not to take pictures. Photographs are taken by special teams from the host. In that vein, the personal information of the guest has been withheld.

This is at the top of some of my favorite letters I have ever received:

With an event such as this, you sort of anticipate emotional moments. Unexpectedly, the first things to grab my heart were hands. Hands flapping excitedly and a young man toe-jumping in the air at the entrance of the banquet room. For me, it was the immediate knowing, the instant recognition deep down, of the something that makes this young man and my own daughter, Rhema, so dear and beautiful and unique. It was gladness for his gladness, and appreciation for all the effort he'd made to be there.

So it goes, in God's economy, the ones who intend to help/volunteer/bless others are the ones who get doubly blessed in return.

I once said that when you have a child with special needs, every child with special needs is your child. I'm not sure that's right, but sometimes it feels that way. I'm sensitive to some of the struggles and sorrows and triumphs and joys of others as if they were my own children. I'm liable to get weepy at the grocery store when I see a man with special needs doing his job and loving his job and touching the lives of the people around him.

So perhaps you can imagine my joy, multiplied by one hundred, seeing our guests lavishly loved and treasured and honored with a night that was made just for them.

There have been times I've wanted to shout

to everyone and no one in particular, "Don't forget my girl. It's not easy, I know. But she's here, sitting in the dark, waiting for you to sit with her, see her, know her. Don't forget my girl."

At Night to Shine, God whispered to me, "I will never ever forget her. She is famous to Me like an A-lister walking the red carpet. I throw a party, serve the best food, and clothe her in love. I pamper her with My goodness and put a crown on her head. She is precious, and she is Mine."

How extravagant is the love of God for us.

God loves us. He does not forget us. There is no one who sits in the dark, alone, that He doesn't see. In His omniscience, God's vision surpasses our own, and He partners with us to bring that light and glory to earth so His name can be known.

The same is true for you. The impact you make will be worth every ounce of effort, every minute of work, and every question and challenge you are likely going to face.

Take heart; God is in it with you.

God Knows

Ever since he can remember, Daniel used to watch the skies in Burkina Faso in West Africa. Standing in the yard of the orphanage in which he lived, he'd gaze out into the vast expanse of blue. As weightless clouds drifted by, he'd look this way and that, hoping for a sign of an airplane. Whenever Daniel would spot a moving speck of gray or hear the familiar hum of a jet engine, his eyes would widen. And he'd wonder the same thing every time. Every day. For years. **Is that my parents coming to get me?** It never was.

At least not the mom and dad he expected.

When Lisa and Shawn Strutz were raising their three children in Wisconsin, Lisa partnered with a ministry at her church that serves and advocates for orphans and widows in Burkina Faso. At the time, Lisa was regularly sent profiles, including pictures of some of the children. Often, she would hold on to the pictures and pray over them. One rainy afternoon, Lisa was at a track meet for her oldest son. She sat with her daughter and other son huddled under an umbrella. A stranger passed by, looked at them, and asked the most peculiar thing: "Can I take a picture of you and your children? I want you to see what I see." Though reluctant at such an unusual request, Lisa agreed and offered the man her phone. After he snapped the picture and left, she and her kids laughed at the photo and the incident and began scrolling through her phone.

"Who's that?" her son asked, pointing to a boy he didn't know. It turned out to be a picture of a ten-year-old boy from Burkina Faso, one of the children whose profiles Lisa had saved. This boy had permanent optical-nerve damage and would be later diagnosed with polymicrogyria and anxiety and found to be on the autism spectrum. He was waiting for a forever family. Then, even odder than the stranger's wanting to take the family's picture, Lisa's son blurted out, "He should be my brother." Many months later, Lisa would look back and remember that picture as Daniel's birth into their family.

It took twenty-three months for the Strutzes to welcome Daniel into his new home in Wisconsin. That's almost two years of being obedient and following God's lead, as well as sometimes questioning what they were doing and why they were doing it. For example, after sending in their final payment to the adoption agency, they received a call that the agency had filed for bankruptcy. Not only was their money gone, but their channel to Daniel was destroyed. To Lisa's knowledge at the time, that organization was the only agency in the entire United States with a protocol to facilitate adoption from Burkina Faso. The Strutz family was crushed. According to Lisa, "Daniel had been told he had a family waiting for him, and we were desperate to keep our promise to him." They didn't know how or when. While doubt would occasionally steal their attention, they trusted God would fulfill this mission. Lisa would ultimately partner with our organization so she could bring Daniel home. Their road to Daniel had snaked through twists and turns, obstacles they had no way in their own strength and knowledge of overcoming. And yet, as Lisa told me,

God showed up . . . again and again. He opened one door after the next. In hindsight, He had been working behind the scenes for so many years before. This has been so faithfully lived out in our family. Our marriage nearly broke, and we have been tested the past five years to the brink, but we have had a front-row seat to redemption: Daniel's and ours. That terrified little boy has grown into a beautiful six-foot-three-inch African man who trusts us (not without reassurance some days). He has learned to treat our family pets and his sisters with compassion. He **loves** Jesus. I mean, **loves.** He is an infectious light to everyone who meets him, and we are the fortunate ones who get to love him through it.

God didn't give us all the answers up front because ultimately we are walking in relationship with Him. He is so faithful to equip us if we are willing to trust Him in it, around it, and through it.

Recently, Lisa was listening to a song, half paying attention to the lyrics. A line jumped out at her, something about the artist not needing her name in lights because she was already famous in God's eyes. The melodic words gave her pause. She began to reflect on a conversation she'd had the other evening with another mother of a child with special needs:

We shared how tiring it can be some days not to have affection reciprocated. We talked about endless analytics, it seems, trying to figure out what's **really** underneath the behavior and how darn hard it is not to take it personally some days. As I listened to this song, these questions burned into my heart: **Am I really okay with God having glory in my son's life? Am I okay with doing all this hard work for essentially no recognition from him? Am I okay with him living his life as if I wasn't the one supplying his needs?** As we continued talking, we both admitted and choked on the "had we known" question. If we would have known how hard this would have been and how much it would stretch **every single ugly thing** inside of us, would we have done it?

And then Jesus whispered in my ear and said, **But I did know. I knew all those dark places of your heart. I knew you would live life as if I am not supplying your every need. I knew you would curse Me some days and give Me joy on a few others. I knew you would struggle and pull and cry out. And I knew you and I could do this,**

for My glory and his redemption. And I chose you so willingly.

Wow! What a powerful truth. You don't have to know everything right now. God already does. Sometimes we feel ill equipped or unworthy or undeserving to do what we feel He is calling us to do. He knows the plans He has for you, so do it anyway.

If you feel uncertain as to where to start, let's start small and take it to ground level. What does God's Word ask you to do? While portions of the Bible are difficult to understand, as there are so many schools of thought on prophecies and the book of Revelation and the Trinity, some of the easier parts to comprehend revolve around what we as believers are called to do. I, for one, am so glad God made that practical.

Help the needy? Love? Defend the defenseless? Be merciful? Yes to all those things.

It's okay to feel afraid or have questions while taking the first step. Do it anyway. Just keep moving the ball five yards. And five more yards. And five more.

In the Great Commission, Jesus told His followers to "go, therefore, and make disciples of all the nations" (see Matthew 28:18–20). You don't have to take a ten-hour flight and do that where you land. Do it as you go. Do it as you wash dishes and raise your children. Do it as your purchases are being rung up at a convenience store. Do it as you style a magazine photo shoot. Do it on the trading floor. Be the light Jesus has been to you wherever you may be.

We are called to love God and to love people. The best definition of the verb form of **love** that I know is to choose the best interest of another person over your own and act on his or her behalf. Let's find people who are in need and act on their behalf.

When you are willing to be used by God, He will open your eyes to opportunities to step in and fill a gap. It's okay to feel afraid or have questions while taking the first step. Do it anyway. Just keep moving the ball five yards. And five more yards. And five more.

Once you spark movement, it will always lead to another opportunity, and another, and another after that.

But it always starts with one step.

Are you ready to take that step?

6

PURPOSE IN THE RESISTANCE

It is doubtful whether God can bless a man greatly until he has hurt him deeply.
—A. W. Tozer

WEIGHING BARELY FOUR POUNDS, Manuel Alfredo, nicknamed Alfredito, was born two months early in October 2003 in his home of Guatemala. His parents, Irene and Alfredo Salazar, and their two daughters couldn't wait to take him home when he was finally discharged after a one-month stay in the neonatal ICU. Alfredito brought much joy to his family. Although his growth and neurological development were slightly below average because he was premature, he was a happy and sweet baby.

When Alfredito was eight months old, his grandfather sensed that something was unique apart from the standard complications of a premature birth.

At the man's persistent urging, Irene and Alfredo took their son to another pediatrician for an evaluation. This doctor performed a physical and neurological examination on Alfredito. His findings—and the way he delivered them—proved devastating to the parents. The doctor told the Salazars that Alfredito had Down syndrome. Without pausing to allow the Salazars to process this curveball, the doctor proceeded to scold them for not knowing this and thereby being eight months behind on tests and treatment that would progress Alfredito's development. The Salazars were dumbfounded. They left the doctor's office that day in tears. Trying to process the unexpected news, they sat in their car in the parking lot, fielding questions they couldn't answer: **How could we have missed this? What does this mean for Alfredito? How will our lives change? What are we going to do? What should we do next?**

What seemed worse than the startling diagnosis was the response they received when they first shared the news with a family member. One woman immediately burst into tears and said, "Why did God do this to you? You serve Him." Her sorrow made them feel as though Alfredito were a mistake, an infant whose value had deteriorated because of a medical label that had just been slapped on him. Although many people reacted to the baby's diagnosis quietly or apologetically, there were others who offered more positivity. One such person was a rabbi the Salazars had recently met through a mutual friend.

"Congratulations," he told them. "Alfredito will teach you many things." Though fear gnawed at their spirits, the Salazars trusted God, believing there was a greater purpose at hand in this diagnosis.

When Alfredito was a year old, another devastating blow arrived. Doctors discovered five defects in his heart that demanded open-heart surgery. The operation was rescheduled multiple times for a variety of reasons. In an act of desperation, the family came to the United States for treatment. A doctor performed an echocardiogram on Alfredito and told his parents that additional tests were required because his condition was more serious than they thought and some arteries could be permanently damaged, initially casting some doubt over whether the surgery could be performed. But a few days later, the doctor confirmed that surgery was still a viable medical option, but because the Salazars did not have insurance, it was a cost-prohibitive option. The American doctor suggested that the family go back to their homeland and seek care there.

The Salazars returned to Guatemala with new concerns and new hopes. But then a miracle happened. The hospital back home scheduled and completed Alfredito's surgery. The little boy recovered brilliantly and was released in good health after a week in the hospital.

During the frustrating time prior to Alfredito's surgery, the Salazars had a revelation. Their eyes were opened to the world of special needs. They began to meet other parents of children with Down syndrome. When they were in the United States, they saw people with Down syndrome living a full life, working and going to school. This brought the couple hope. They also discovered the positive impact that supportive environments had on these children. Conversely, they observed that the children who did not receive therapy and whose parents did not work with them deteriorated developmentally. The couple was beginning to understand the needs and particularly the gaps in support systems for those with Down syndrome where they lived. It wasn't just Alfredito who needed support; there were countless others who deserved the same.

With Purpose Comes Sacrifice

One night, Alfredo felt God impressing a truth in his heart that he couldn't shake. In his spirit, he heard first the truth that He loves the parents of children with Down syndrome just as He loves their children. He felt God telling him to share this love and to support these parents as they worked with their children to help them achieve optimal development. Alfredo didn't realize the magnitude of this mission at the time, but it was this whisper that began to change the way he and his wife saw their future.

In 2005, the Salazars founded Down Guatemala, an organization that provides support, education, and therapy to children with Down syndrome in Guatemala City. At the time, there were almost no organizations like it in their country. The couple didn't have much money, so they sold the home they had recently purchased to fund the ministry, securing a location and staff. In a country where more than half the population lives below the poverty line, with an average salary of $435 a month, the families served by Down Guatemala needed this new organization's assistance. In light of this poverty and the lack of government assistance, the Salazars' mission was to provide early intervention training for families as well as adaptive programs specialized to best serve the needs of children with Down syndrome.

When the couple made the biggest sacrifice of selling their home, they had high expectations:

> We thought that many people would support us financially once they saw what a great cause it was to support people with a disability. Unfortunately, it was not like that. It cost us many family sacrifices to keep the organization open.

Receiving minimal donations, the couple continued to provide from their own pockets and resources. They sold whatever possessions they had, including their cars. They spent every dime of their savings to keep the organization alive. After a year and a half of serving twenty-two families five days a week, it looked as though they would have to shut down their mission.

A mission-possible life is often marked by miracles. This might look like deep fulfillment and inexplicable peace in the clutch of hardship. Or it might be the opportunity to witness the hand of God in impossible situations and see Him do what we cannot.

But God loves to manifest miracles when we're vulnerable, when there are reasons we need them. It's usually when we've put ourselves in positions of discomfort on purpose: when we give up something now for something greater and that will last; when we choose studying over scrolling; when we choose to give our money to a cause rather than buy jeans we don't need; when we choose to train instead of snooze; when we choose to be uncomfortable.

> **When we live mission possible, sacrifice is inevitable. It's a fixed numeral in the equation. Our lives may even be defined to some degree by the level of sacrifices we are willing to make.**

A life of significance is steeped in sacrifice. The Salazars were willing to sacrifice their material possessions, even necessities like a car, for a mission they believed in. It got uncomfortable for them. But that's what happens when we sacrifice. The balance is much lower than what makes us feel secure. The work seems overwhelming, and the time is never enough. But when we live mission possible and put the needs of others before ourselves, we are invited to see not what is **us** possible but what is only **God** possible.

The Salazars' season of desperation and scarcity proved to be an opportunity for them to strengthen their faith. Their sacrifices blossomed into a sequence of miracles that broke through many eleventh hours. Over the years, Down Guatemala received unexpected and large donations from Alfredo's employer and Target stores, as well as partnerships with Orphan Outreach and our foundation. When I met them and saw their organization at work, I knew in my heart they were something special. Irene and Alfredo were kind, and it was clear their hearts were in the right place. They believed in what they were doing, and it showed in how they led and served the organization.

In October 2020, Down Guatemala celebrated its fifteenth anniversary. The organization has served more than 350 families, of which 65 percent are Indigenous (of Mayan descent) and have access to zero resources. Irene Salazar told me,

We have learned as a family that serving the vulnerable—being the voice of the voiceless, fighting for those who can't fight for themselves—is one of the greatest privileges we have.

This process has been of continuous learning not to depend on men, not to depend on any organization, but to depend on God at all times.

We have realized that everything we have on this earth does not belong to us. We are only administrators of it, and if the owner, who is God, asks you to give it, you must give it with joy. He is the owner, and He knows what is best for our lives and our ministries.

Many years ago, if someone had asked me who our biggest donor was, I would have answered, "Target." In 2016, they gave us their final donation. That year, I understood that our main donor is the Lord, and it is He who brings the donors and so we must depend on Him.

My family and I many times have felt just like the people of Israel, who heard the voice of God and went out to the desert to try to reach the Promised Land. We left our home, a place where we had relative comfort, to go to the middle of nowhere to learn how to depend on God.

Like the Israelites, we have seen His favor when we have needed something. And He has always provided.

When the Israelites arrived at the Promised Land, they had to fight to conquer the different cities that had been promised to them.

We have learned that to achieve the promises God has made about the ministry, we, too, must fight. We fight against our thoughts, our doubts, and our unbelief. But, praise God, He has always given us the victory!

The Christian life is built on sacrifice. God gave His only Son so we can live with Him for eternity. I love the beauty with which Alfredo wrapped this undeniable truth around the context of the ministry he and his wife built. This is what he said:

If you really want to build something, you are going to have to sacrifice something.

The greatest ministry that has existed in history is the ministry of salvation. This was God's plan for humanity, and to achieve it, He had to sacrifice the most precious thing He had: His very own Son.

Every time we see in the Bible that God gave people instructions to develop great projects, they had to sacrifice great things in their lives.

The size of the sacrifice is not proportional to the size of the victory; the success is almost always much larger.

Sacrifice is the greatest example of love that

we have. Only when you really love something with all your heart are you willing to sacrifice yourself or sacrifice something that you possess.

In our case, we have had to sacrifice much: our house and four vehicles. We have also had to apply for three big bank loans. Much of my salary went directly to the ministry. And we sacrificed time with our family, including vacations. Today we still do not have a house of our own, but that is no longer important.

When you sacrifice things out of love, it doesn't hurt, and you are not waiting for the moment when they will return.

Sacrifice is not the most pleasing word. For many of us, it brings to mind the need to give it all up or to give until it hurts. While making sacrifices may not feel as good as a nap in a onesie on a cold rainy day, there are benefits to it. One study published in **Social Psychological and Personality Science** trumpeted that greater happiness is found when we deny ourselves, even temporarily, something pleasurable, like chocolate bars.[1] When we live mission possible, sacrifice is inevitable. It's a fixed numeral in the equation. Our lives may even be defined to some degree by the level of sacrifices we are willing to make. Rather than looking at sacrifice as a negative marker or something we feel tempted to resist, we should see it as something we ought to embrace.

Viktor Frankl's book **Man's Search for Meaning** teaches us that sacrifice can be transformative, the purpose-making difference in our lives. In his book, he shared his experience in the Holocaust and how he was able to survive the brutal horrors of a Nazi concentration camp and the loss of almost everyone he loved, including his pregnant wife. He posits that humans are able to endure the worst of circumstances when it is connected to a sense of purpose. In one of my favorite passages, Frankl wrote, "In some way, suffering ceases to be suffering at the moment it finds a meaning, such as the meaning of a sacrifice."[2]

> ## The true meaning of sacrifice: giving up what you want now for what you want most.

I doubt that the Salazars were outright excited about having to sell their car or the home they loved, but I know that when they were able to help the first family who walked through their doors, the contribution paled in comparison to the reward. They know the true meaning of sacrifice: giving up what you want now for what you want most.

Go Ahead, Get Uncomfortable

One of the greatest enemies of living a mission-possible life is the pursuit of comfort. French scientist Alexis de Tocqueville came to the United States in 1831 to write a big book called **Democracy in America.** After conducting more than two hundred interviews and visiting seventeen states in nine months, he wrote over eight hundred pages on what he saw was the most democratic and flourishing nation on earth. In an essay titled "On the Taste for Material Well-Being in America," de Tocqueville noted in a less than complimentary manner that those living in the United States "are universally preoccupied with meeting the body's every need and attending to life's little comforts."[3]

Dang!

Remember, the Frenchman wrote this in 1831. This was a time absent of smartphones and smart cars and Google and washing machines and drive-throughs and Postmates and overnight shipping and online banking and virtual education and telemedicine. Still, Americans were nevertheless focused on making themselves as comfortable as possible. Wow. Could you imagine what he'd have to say now? I'm sort of embarrassed that de Tocqueville's truth bomb detonates with even more power almost two centuries later!

Comfort is, well, comfortable. It's warm and cozy and loves to tempt us to stay longer than we promised ourselves we would. But when we choose, and keep choosing, to sacrifice a mission-possible life for the path of least resistance, we actually suffer. We stop growing. Sure, we may experience less stress and more predictability, but we also miss out on untapped adventures. We squash any opportunity to challenge and strengthen our faith. We abandon the potential to live what Jesus wanted for each one of us: an abundant life. Sometimes you just have to be the first one to get uncomfortable, especially when everyone is watching.

For parts of my life, one of the things I was most passionate about and willing to sacrifice for was sports. I'd be the first one up and the last one to go to sleep. I'd wake up at midnight sometimes just to train because I knew no one else was doing it. I didn't mind making myself uncomfortable on purpose if it meant I would gain greater physical ability or the respect of my teammates. I love what financial guru Dave Ramsey has said: "If you will live like no one else, later you can live like no one else."[4] Sometimes you just have to make a statement in order to do this.

During one of my first few weeks my freshman year at the University of Florida, our coaches and trainers led us in one of our first major workouts, called the Harley-Davidson. I think one of their goals was to manipulate our brains into never giving in and never giving up. I've heard Mickey Marotti, our legendary strength coach back in the day, has since backed off a bit, but when we Gators trained under him, he showed us no mercy. One day, my teammates and I worked our muscles into overtime with sled pushes until our legs couldn't move another inch, wall squats until our muscles quivered into useless piles of Jell-O, and tug-of-war battles in which the rope ended up coated in the blood from our hands. I'm pretty sure most of us were puking by the time we were done.

As if that weren't enough, while we were still wiping the vomit off our lips, our trainers had more marching orders on their agenda.

"Get in the cold tub and start recovering. All of you. Up to your hips. Just seven minutes. Let's go!" Ice baths, a form of cryotherapy, are highly beneficial for athletes. They decrease soreness, reduce swelling and muscle damage, and speed recovery so you can push it harder the next workout or game or race. They're also completely not fun. No one wants to do them. They're just not natural.

My teammates and I gathered around the tubs in the room. I stood by as they looked at the freezing water. They pointed at the tubs. They started talking and complaining about them. They did just about everything but actually get in the tubs.

"Let's go!" a voice from the training room bellowed. Our coaches and trainers were in a room right in front of the cold-tub room, which had a window so they could monitor our progress. "Gotta get in for seven minutes. Move!"

My teammates, some of the biggest and baddest ballers I knew, were freaking out. There was more talking, but no one moved. But after more yelling from the training room, a few of the guys stepped into a tub and got in maybe to their knees, yapping and yelling the farther they dipped themselves into the ice-cold water.

"Get your hips in, guys. Let's go!"

After watching everyone complain and joke and continue to resist what they were going to have to do eventually, I quietly stepped aside from the crowd and took a few steps forward to the cold tub. Without saying a word, I crept inside. My toes immediately contracted. Sinking deeper as I squatted into the tub, my body instinctively recoiled over and over from the freezing temperature. Muscles stung. Skin burned. Although I needed to plunge my body only up to my hips, I dipped farther into the frigid tub of agony until only my head bobbed out of the water. On the inside, I was dying, my skin frozen in shock. To everyone on the outside, my poker face was on point. It was a walk in the park. **Yawn.**

This was a mission. See, I didn't want to just get the guys to like me; I needed them to respect me. Respect in the game is more important than being liked. If they respect me, then they'll play hard for me. Sure, part of this had to do with ego. I needed the guys to think of me as a different kind of animal who looked at pain differently. But this was also an opportunity to set the tone of who I was and what I was about. It was a sign of my character—evidence, however small, that I was willing to go to the nth degree to get uncomfortable for something greater.

Making a big deal out of getting in a cold tub may seem silly to you, but I gained cred that day. I was willing to put myself in an uncomfortable position because I wanted people to look at me differently so that one day they would play for me differently. I knew that if my teammates respected me for being the first to get uncomfortable and going the extra mile, then they would reciprocate that same effort for me one day. I was so passionate about leading by example because I wanted to be a great quarterback. I wanted to be a great leader. I wanted to have an impact on my teammates. I wanted them to follow me, so I had to step out and be a little bit different, and sometimes it meant I had to do things that made me uncomfortable. I didn't want to get into an ice-cold tub up to my neck. But I would gladly do it again if I could have an impact on my teammates so they could think, **That guy is doing anything he can, so I might go a little bit further to do what I can too.**

Oh, yeah, it was definitely cold. But here's a tip. If you get through the first two and a half minutes, the rest is easy. That's true of almost every good hard thing, isn't it? The toughest part is almost always starting.

I believe that every single one of us has that choice. We can do something difficult and uncomfortable that stretches us and doesn't feel good, because we know there are greater gains. When's the last time you had an opportunity to show others who you really are by getting uncomfortable?

Is It a Setback or a Setup?

When we live saturated with purpose, we ought not to be blindsided by the enemies that slip into our minds and block our paths—enemies like comfort and convenience and fearing the unknown. It shouldn't surprise us when obstacles try to stake their claim on whatever missions we're trying to accomplish. In 1 Corinthians 16:8–9, Paul wrote a telling statement: "I will stay in Ephesus until Pentecost, for a wide door for effective work has opened to me, and there are many adversaries" (ESV). **The Message** has a pithy way of saying it: "A huge door of opportunity for good work has opened up here. (There is also mushrooming opposition.)"

Paul was writing this from the city of Ephesus. He had planned to stay there until Pentecost but ended up staying longer. During his stay, many people came to know that Jesus and Paul performed many miracles. But because of its success, Paul's ministry aroused dangerous enemies who tried to ruin the good he was doing and destroy him. Not everyone was a fan of Paul's rising influence. At the time of his writing 1 Corinthians, Paul most likely had no idea that this "mushrooming opposition" would result in a riot in Ephesus and cause him to depart for Macedonia (see Acts 19:23–20:1). In other passages, he described his opposition as fighting with wild beasts and as an excessive burden (see 1 Corinthians 15:32; 2 Corinthians 1:8). Paul didn't let the resistance deter him from his mission, however. In fact, he doubled down. He exerted himself in sharing the gospel with even more passion. He used the "mushrooming opposition" to further ignite his mission.

Human beings were created with a fight-or-flight response. This is an innate physiological reaction that sets in motion when we're threatened or under attack. In simple terms, we're wired to handle stress. I'm not saying we should live in such a way that induces chronic stress. Chronic stress will absolutely take a toll on an individual. We're talking high blood pressure, sleep issues, heart disease, mental ailments, cancer. However, biologically speaking, our body's stress response was designed to help us maintain our well-being and meet the demands of survival. Researchers at Berkeley have found that some stress can actually be good for you. Daniela Kaufer, associate professor of integrative biology, has discovered that short-lived stress actually "primes the brain for improved performance."[5] This is referred to as stress-related growth, or physiological thriving.

Ms. Kaufer is not alone in her findings. Research indicates that stress can affect our well-being in a positive way if we have the right perspective. Viktor Frankl knew what he was talking about.

When our foundation chooses employees, one of the essentials we look for is whether they have had to deal with strong resistance or hardship in the execution of their missions. Same with our business partnerships. We want to understand if and how they endured something tough. Did they stay the course? Did they remain faithful? Did the opposition make them better, create more wisdom in them, or prepare them for the next battle? We want to partner with people who have faced strong resistance and experienced growth through it. It's one of the most telling attributes of what relationships will thrive in the long term.

What challenges are you facing today as you strive to live mission possible? Has the pandemic forced you to stop, rethink, and restart a plan for your life, your dream, or your family? Maybe you're tired of constantly having to sacrifice your time or money, and the payoff doesn't seem to exceed, let alone equal, the work. Take a breath. Don't give up. If you quit, you will never know what tomorrow held. You will never know where that breakthrough was going to be. You don't know the doors that are just about to open for you. You never know what you're going to miss out on.

When COVID-19 took life as we knew it into custody, I lost a baseball season, a dream I may never get back. But many other people lost a lot more:

their health, their businesses, even their loved ones. When I first learned that baseball was canceled, my natural response was stress. I definitely felt that knot in my stomach. But what looked like a setback actually turned out to be a setup for incredible opportunities I never would have had. Had I been on the road, I wouldn't have spent as much time with my new bride. We wouldn't have welcomed three fur babies into our home (Chunk, Kobe, and Paris). I wouldn't have been a part of the hiring process for many new employees.

When you flip your perspective on the uncomfortable, you may find that a setback can look a lot more like a setup. Think about it this way. If the journey of Daniel from the Bible didn't include his suffering from being taken from his homeland, assimilated into a new culture, and getting his character attacked, there probably wouldn't have been a chance for him to shine at his greatest moment facing the lions. The same can be said about Joseph. If Joseph wasn't betrayed by his own brothers, by his boss's wife, and by his coworkers, who knows if he would have had a chance to be the second-most-powerful man in Egypt and be in such a position to help his starving family. If the stakes weren't so high for Queen Esther, she wouldn't have been in the position to save an entire nation of people.

If you are struggling with an addiction, on the verge of a relationship collapse, or going through a painful or unimaginable situation, allow me to encourage you. God uses people who are wounded and have been broken. Those are some of the best candidates to live mission-possible lives.

Just look at the above examples again. None of those individuals had an easy go in life. They suffered. They were betrayed. They were persecuted. I imagine in those pressing times of hardship, they probably even questioned God's plan. I can't tell you the expiration date for the crisis that is causing your fears and questions to overflow, but I can remind you that you can do all things through Christ who strengthens you (see Philippians 4:13).

When we embrace the resistance and consider interruptions in our progress as opportunities, we gain greater strength and endurance. We build up stamina to continue to run the race. This is similar to what happens when we work out. When we exercise our muscles, they get microtears. When we keep exercising consistently, the microtears accumulate to form muscle mass. In a sense, our bodies have to be broken down to come back stronger. The same can be true of our lives. Maybe it's time to start looking at setbacks not as dead ends but as detours to take us to greater destinations.

Remember the Big Picture: Eternity

Paul didn't numb out on palm wine or streaming TV because of the magnitude of resistance he faced; he embraced it. And he knew a little secret: "Our momentary, light affliction is producing for us an eternal weight of glory far beyond all comparison, while we look not at the things which are seen, but at the things which are not seen; for the things which are seen are temporal, but the things which are not seen are eternal" (2 Corinthians 4:17–18). Paul knew that there is more to life than what we see.

When you live mission possible, you are investing in eternity. You may not get to play a lot of video games when you live mission possible, and you may find yourself giving up the job that pays the most in order to take the one that's more meaningful, but your fulfillment will be earth shattering. Live today and each day forward with a forever mindset. Focus on doing things that will leave a legacy after you're gone. Keep in mind the words of Alfredo Salazar, who sacrificed not only for his son but for hundreds of families:

> The rewards on earth are many, but the one that fills us the most is knowing that one day the Lord will tell us, "Good and faithful servant, come and enter into the joy of your Lord" for having taken the talents He gave us and multiplying them for the blessing of many people.

Remember Daddy's Dollars? After a few years of doing my best to get the most dollars and by doing things like helping my neighbor with his chicken farm, by the time I was around ten years old, I had a lot of money saved. (At least in the perspective of a little kid.)

By watching some of my siblings, I learned quickly to save the cash and not spend it. I'd seen too often one of them rush out to buy a video game or a cool shirt and then have little or no money left over. I had also watched my dad work tirelessly to help the people he served in the Philippines. I learned early on what a lucky little boy I was. Unlike some of the children served by Dad and his team, I always had something to eat. I had a roof over my head. I had shoes on my feet. I had a mom and a dad. It broke my heart to see children who didn't have those things. I wanted to do something about it, but I was a kid. I didn't have much, but I wanted to use what I had—at the time, the accumulation of Daddy's Dollars—to make a difference. I was determined to use the money I had saved for good.

The Bible tells us that faith, hope, and love will last for all time and that the greatest of these is love. Is there any better way to show Jesus to others than to give to them, serve them, or help them? Doing so is a form of love, and it is something that will have an eternal impact.

Don't run from the resistance. |

As a boy, I dreamed of one day making a million dollars and giving it away. But at the time, all I had were the Daddy's Dollars I had earned, and I always gave my dad some of **that** money to bring with him to the Philippines. I wanted to help kids who didn't have much. Dad would always come back from his trips and tell me story after story about how even my chump change was enough to buy a little boy or girl my age a pair of flip-flops, a bag of food for the child's family, or even a Bible. Even though it probably would have been more fun to buy a video game with that money, I was beginning to understand what it meant to live a mission-possible life. It's about making a difference, loving the least of these, fighting for those who can't fight for themselves. And I wanted to do more of it.

At the time of this writing, Alfredito is seventeen years old. He is a swim star and has even won a bronze medal in the Latin American games of the Special Olympics. And true to the rabbi's words, this young man teaches his parents so many things every day. Alfredito's diagnosis may have changed the plans his parents had for their future, but it's been for the better! And it has also changed the lives of hundreds of others and their families by them having an opportunity to lock arms with Down Guatemala.

Don't run from the resistance.

Remember, there is always a purpose to the pain.

7

ELEVATE CONVICTIONS
OVER EMOTIONS

**Though our feelings come and go,
[God's] love for us does not.**
—C. S. Lewis

WHEN YOU STAND IN FRONT OF A
$1.5 billion mixed-use mega complex that's glisten-
ing in the Texas sun, you can't help but feel that
you are standing in the presence of greatness. The
Star's ninety-one acres hold the no-expense-spared
corporate headquarters and entertainment complex
of the Dallas Cowboys. From the highway, you can
make out the forty-foot-tall light display, a custom
architectural beauty that glimmers in the central
atrium. Anchored by the luxury Omni Hotel and
the Ford Center, a state-of-the-art twelve-thousand-
seat indoor arena that houses the NFL team as well

as eight high school teams, this development is Jerry Jones's version of Disney World.

I touched down in Texas that morning because I was scheduled to speak that evening at the Omni. At the time, I didn't even realize that the hotel was part of the Cowboys' complex. It was a cool coincidence, and it was fun to tour the facilities before the event. The facilities were breathtaking. Every turn down every hallway and into every room made my jaw drop even farther. I mean, have you ever seen a football-shaped locker room? Or a hot tub the size of your neighbor's swimming pool? The exercise facility that was open to guests (guests!) was even better than some of the NFL weight rooms I'd been in over the years.

I was psyched to be able to encourage a couple hundred people later that night at a speaking event, but as I walked around the gargantuan complex that gleamed and sparkled, I felt myself drifting farther and farther away from the excitement of the coming function. That would have been a good thing had it been because I was completely present in the moment, enjoying my tour of the Star. But that wasn't it.

I wasn't distracted because I was spending time worrying about the future, either. And I wasn't worrying about my message or where I was supposed to be or what time or with whom. Here's what took me out of that moment and out of my excitement: where I **was** was reminding me of where I **wasn't**.

The Reality of Our Feelings

My spirit dipped, deeper and deeper, little by little, the farther into the tour I walked. What started out as a **Wow! This is so cool!** sentiment began to shift into a lower gear. The feelings and thoughts that followed centered around unmet longings. Dreams unfulfilled. Questions that I may never have answers to. It felt like a movie in which the voice of the person giving me the amazing guided tour dulled into the background. I saw his gestures pointing to the incredible team-meeting room and the all-digital war room, where the scouting and draft action happens. I was no doubt impressed by what I was being shown, but my emotions began to run interference. They grabbed the mic and began spitting out a wish list of the sour variety.

I wish I had a chance to be a player in this facility.

I wish I had what they have.

I wish I would have . . .

I wish I did . . .

Then came the finger pointing.

God, I wish You had a different plan.

Seeing the Cowboys' facilities made me miss football. Those facilities reminded me of what I didn't have—or, rather, what I wasn't playing. And with those two ingredients simmering in my spirit, I found myself starting to tap into this strange mixture of depression, selfishness, bitterness, and envy.

I hated it. I try to be a pretty good gatekeeper of negative feelings, but those crashed the party. It happened so fast I didn't even have time to check their IDs.

I found myself inwardly in a funk right until the moment I walked onstage at the event hours later and was able to speak to a group of amazing people. My joy was diminished up until that moment because I had fixed my focus on what I **didn't** have. That's not how I wanted that day to go. My intentions weren't to be bitter; my mission that day was to have an impact on a bunch of souls and give hope to those who needed it. Instead, I was totally caught off guard by this emotional sucker punch.

Have you ever had a similar experience? Have you ever taken an emotional hit out of nowhere? Maybe you found yourself turning green when you heard the news about your friend's successful business venture, or perhaps you received another wedding invitation in the mail and have yet another reason to long for your own.

Spend five minutes scrolling on your social media feed. See the happy smiles? The filtered faces? The sweet homes? The well-behaved and well-dressed kids? The magical vacations? The new cars? Studies prove that so much of our lives is spent wishing we had what others had. When jealousy or envy or bitterness snake their way into our hearts, they can occupy a space that's not reserved for them and command control of our actions, our days, and even our outlook on life.

Maybe you feel so tired and you dread putting your kids to bed at night because you know the battle that lies ahead. Or maybe you feel hopeless because you have to cut checks to your employees next week and you know the funds in the checking account are insufficient. The fatigue and the anger and the worry and the knots in your stomach seem to speak more loudly than God's whisper reassuring you, "I've got this."

Feelings aren't all negative or a necessary evil. God created us with feelings. There is something transcendent about looking into the eyes of someone you are madly in love with or standing on top of a mountain, out of breath, muscles burning, but you don't care because you are captured by a view familiar only to the eagle. Those experiences evoke deep emotions. It's like Helen Keller said: "The best and most beautiful things in the world cannot be seen or even touched. They must be felt with the heart."[1]

We explode with anger when we watch the world spin with injustice. We cringe with embarrassment when we spill a drink at a fancy function. We nurse grief when we say goodbye to the love of our life. At times, our emotions are singular and pure, and other times, they're mixed—like my feeling nervous and excited at the same time during the first Night to Shine event.

> **Emotions don't get to rule our every decision.**

Emotions are one avenue through which we experience reality. They're not something that can be so easily dismissed. We were born to feel; it's okay to have feelings. I think about my mom: from having the courage to be one of the first parents to homeschool her children, to packing up her family and moving to the Philippines to a mission field, to almost dying because of her high-risk pregnancy with me, to the countless occasions on which she and Dad had no money and no food on the table but believed provision would come. At times, she must have felt overwhelmed, tired, afraid, and stressed out. Though she didn't wallow in those feelings, she definitely had them.

While emotions may be telltale signs of whatever we are facing or struggling with or even trying to numb out, we do not have to assign them the title of CEO. Emotions don't get to rule our every decision.

Choose the Right Wolf

When negative feelings fester and turn into unmanageable thoughts, we tend to remain in that negative place for much longer than we should. Looking back, as bummed out as I felt walking around the

Cowboys' headquarters, I probably didn't need to remain locked into my gloomy feelings for as long as I did. I'm not saying I should have immediately snapped out of that funk. I'm not a robot. I don't think any of us have the power to tap a "Do not disturb" on our feelings so they instantaneously dissipate into oblivion.

While emotions aren't something we can always control, we need to figure out what to do when they hit us in a way that's detrimental to our spirits. You may have heard the legend about the two wolves sometimes attributed to the Cherokee Nation. An old Indian chief is teaching his grandson lessons about life. "There is a fight going on inside me between two wolves. One is evil, full of hatred, greed, anger, jealousy, lies, and selfishness, and the other is good, full of kindness, love, grace, mercy, and humility. The same fight is going on inside of you." The grandson thinks for a minute, then asks the chief, "Which wolf will win?"

"The one you feed," replies his grandfather.

In the stadium that day, I didn't have to invite envy and bitterness into my soul for a cup of bulletproof coffee for breakfast. I could have starved those feelings by focusing on what I did have in the moment: an absolutely amazing opportunity to bless a group of incredible men and women and show appreciation for who they are and what they do. I could have fed those thoughts with my attention.

We have a choice. We always do: we can soak and

bathe in our misery, or we can turn over those un-
ruly emotions to God.

> **The number one defense against the antagonism of feelings is to dive into the Word of God.**

As believers, we have a mechanism available to us
that can keep imposing emotions far enough away
so we can still maintain contentment. His name is
Jesus. He gives us a way out—not out of trouble or
away from upsetting emotions, but out of captivity
to that which can encumber our spirits.

To me, the number one defense against the an-
tagonism of feelings is to dive into the Word of God.
See for yourself the advice the Bible gives:

> Come to Me, all who are weary and bur-
> dened, and I will give you rest. Take My yoke
> upon you and learn from Me, for I am gentle
> and humble in heart, and you will find rest
> for your souls. (Matthew 11:28–29)

On the evening of January 8, 2009, the Florida
Gators would face the Oklahoma Sooners in Miami,
Florida, for the national championship game. I re-
member sitting in my hotel room that afternoon
during the three-hour break Coach Urban gave us.
Nerves churned inside my stomach as I tried to

inhale and exhale deeply to calm my racing heart. I decided to hold an impromptu Bible study. My teammates and also Pastor Lindsey Seals, our chaplain, started filling up the room, one by one, until we reached capacity. The shoulders of each person in that room slumped with so much pressure. Referencing Matthew 11:28–29, I began to try to encourage the guys: "Our weight feels heavy right now, but we have the choice to give it to God, for He is gentle and lowly in heart." Pastor Lindsey brought a guitar and started leading us in worship songs. The experience settled our souls, and we each left the room a little bit lighter and a little bit brighter. That's what happens when we give God what we cannot carry any longer.

Jesus invites, welcomes, and encourages everyone—the weak, the miserable, the overwhelmed, the hopeless, the tired—to "come" to Him. He's receiving those who are waving the white flag in surrender, those who recognize their inability to succeed on their own, the ones who acknowledge their sinfulness and lack of control. For those people, Jesus says, "I will give you rest" (verse 28).

I appreciate what the **Holman New Testament Commentary** notes about this in Matthew:

In that agrarian culture, everyone knew that a **yoke** (11:29, 30) went across the necks of two beasts of burden, just in front of their shoulders, and connected them to the plow or wagon they were to pull. Under the covenant relationship, the believer is not relieved of all work or burden, but is given work that is appropriate to his abilities, within his limitations. In fact, the believer will find the work fulfilling and rewarding rather than toilsome and exhausting. Jesus' yoke is easy (suitable, good, reasonable), and his burden is **light** (easy to bear, insignificant).

Jesus instructed his followers to **take my yoke** at their own initiative. Jesus will not put it on us without our consent. But to refuse Jesus' yoke is not to be burden-free, but to retain a much heavier burden. Everyone in life must carry a burden; the question is whether we will carry one that is within our capacity, or one heavier than we were designed for.

To learn from me goes hand in hand with taking on Jesus' yoke. What Jesus will teach us is how to live under the light burden he offers and to enjoy his rest. As our teacher, he will deal with us with sensitivity and compassion.[2]

First Peter 5:6–7 tells us, "Humble yourselves under the mighty hand of God, so that He may exalt you at the proper time, having cast all your anxiety on Him, because He cares about you." The context around "casting our cares" in this passage is humility. Notice what Peter said first: "Humble yourselves." Under what? "Under the mighty hand of God."

Not your own hand.

Typically, what happens in trying, anxious, and nerve-racking times is that we still attempt to hold on to control. However, we're called to do the opposite. To let go. To humbly submit. The reason it's so hard to cast our cares on the Lord is that our pride gets in the way. Pride is intentionally or un-intentionally thinking more or less of oneself. Either "I got this; I don't need Jesus" or "Why would Jesus want to help a useless waste of space like me?" See, pride isn't just thinking you're a hotshot. Pride is also doubting your self-value and worth, which is the root of most anxiety. Pride can create conceit or feelings of lowliness.

Neither produces righteousness.

Choosing humility produces a holy confidence.

Why would Jesus want to help you? Because He cares for you. Please hear me when I say this: to be cared for does not equate to inferiority; to be cared for is to be loved. And God loves you so much that He wants to take your burdens off your back. To refuse this invitation is foolish and prideful. When we humble ourselves, submitting to the fact that God's got us, only by His doing can we release our cares upon Him. Choosing humility produces a holy confidence.

The Hebrew term used for **cast** means to throw upon someone or something else. This is an intentional, active decision. It's choosing to trust. The same term is used in Psalm 55:22: "**Cast** your burden upon the LORD and He will sustain you." **The Message** paraphrases it, "Pile your troubles on GOD's shoulders—he'll carry your load, he'll help you out."

The Bible doesn't teach us that we will never have burdens. On the contrary, it tells us that we will be persecuted, endure trials, and wage war with darkness. When we're met with stress or crises, it's not because we're awful people who have done something wrong. We're just passing through this time on earth and living in the fallen experience. So the question isn't **if** we will experience hard stuff; it's **how** we will respond. How do we cope with off-kilter emotions that stem from unpleasant situations?

It's simple yet so hard to do at times. We hope. We soak and bathe not in our misery but in the words of Jesus: "These things I have spoken to you so that in Me you may have peace. In the world you have tribulation, but take courage; I have overcome the world" (John 16:33). Casting our burdens and choosing hope is not a onetime deal. When we feel overwhelmed, unhinged, or faint of heart, we cast our cares on Jesus. We do it moment by moment, hour by hour, or minute by minute if we need to.

Today and tomorrow. We choose to cast and keep casting our cares on the One who brought us from death to life.

When Jesus died on the cross for our sins, He gave us the channel to move from the old to the new. The debt we owed was canceled because He took our place. He paid our balance in full. Because of this greatest gift, we can live connected to the Creator of the universe every day. We have a source for everything, including our emotional well-being. We can keep going to Him, and that source will never be broken.

As we cast our cares, we begin to recognize those things that are outside our control, which, technically speaking, are most things. We may not control who hires us, when or why we'll spend a week in the hospital, or if we'll be on the list of layoffs, but we can focus on what we are called to do: live mission possible.

Instead of isolating ourselves, we can love God.

Instead of feeling bitter, we can love people.

Instead of being selfish, we can put the interests of others above our own.

Instead of complaining, we can serve.

Instead of being paralyzed by fear, we can take action.

Instead of being trapped by doubt, we can say yes.

When we begin to realize the unshakable character of God, whatever comes our way, we can stand firm and live by our convictions.

The Power of Conviction

I like how David Jeremiah defined **conviction:** "a fixed belief, a deeply held set of certainties that lodges in the center of your mind and heart."[3]

Convictions aren't merely opinions. They don't change based on your mood or how your kids behave on a certain day or what position you get on the team.

On the other hand, convictions aren't something you default to without taking time to reflect and consider them.

Convictions are intentionally chosen and honed throughout life, particularly through situations that vie for the immediate and total attention of your emotions. They are also something by which you can shape or reshape your perspective.

Belief in providence is just one example of conviction. Can you think of one of your own? What's one core conviction you have?

When you are faced with a choice, your convictions will propel you to do the right thing rather than react to what your feelings are telling you. Sometimes convictions are about perspective.

I believe I'm here on this earth for a reason. I believe that for you too. In fact, that's a conviction I live by—that God has a purpose and a plan for my life and for each and every person on this earth. I believe that even when I'm tired or struggling with making the right decisions.

I have learned that convictions are stronger than emotions. Emotions will lie to you. Emotions will tell you in the morning when your alarm goes off that you're too tired, that you didn't get enough sleep, that you deserve to snooze, that you'll get up early tomorrow for real this time. But if you listen to your convictions, regardless of what your emotions feed you to get you to do what they want, you'll be the first one up. You'll be the last one standing. You'll run through the pain. You'll keep building the boat even when the sky is clear. You'll do things you may not necessarily want to because it puts the interests of others before your own.

Demi and I share many common interests: our faith, for one. We also love spending time with family and are both health conscious. But we also have our differences. For starters, she loves dressing up and going out to dinner. She relishes the ambience, takes her sweet time carefully choosing what to order, savors a glass of wine, admires the presentation of her entrée, and soaks up every minute of the outing. I, on the other hand, couldn't care less about going out on the town. I'm on the road, at least pre-COVID-19, all the time, so when I have free time, I want to enjoy my Zevia and the food in my kitchen—or what's delivered—in the comfort and privacy of my own home. But if there's one thing I've learned in my many years of marriage (#sarcasm), it's that my feelings are not my only priority. The second I said "I do," I signed up for more than my emotions. Just because I put a ring on Demi's finger doesn't mean I should stop courting her. I live by the conviction that I love her and that instead of doing whatever I want all the time, I want to serve her in ways that matter to her. I take a drive even when I'm tired. I go to a restaurant even when I feel like staying in. I walk along a beach even though I hate sand. I do all these things for Demi, and though I wouldn't usually get joy from the activities themselves, I am happy, truly, because my wife is happy. And that brings me joy as well.

I don't get it right every time with Demi. Sometimes when I live by my convictions, I have to make a decision between two good choices. I remember one time when I had to choose between doing two good and important things for people I loved. That was plain awful. I was walking out of a huge pro-life event in Waco, Texas, just before midnight one evening. I had missed a number of calls from my sister Katie. One of her daughters had been crying for hours, asking her if I could come speak at a Special Person Day event at her school the next day. My mom was supposed to attend but couldn't because of a last-minute schedule conflict. I was supposed to be filming live at 11 a.m. for **SEC Nation** that same day but quickly made some last-minute arrangements to fly to Atlanta for my niece's event. She was thrilled. Her tears had dried, and I felt honored to step into the gap for my mother that morning.

I almost broke every law trying to get to the airport on time so I could make a televised appearance for **SEC Nation.** I sprinted up to the stage at, no joke, 10:59 a.m. There was so much scheduling and replanning in such a short time that I didn't consider that Demi, my fiancée at the time, had really, really wanted to get in a premarital counseling session the same morning I had chosen to speak at my niece's school. Understandably, she felt disappointed and underappreciated because I didn't make myself available to her.

There are times when your conviction to do the right thing requires discernment and wisdom, especially if you have multiple good opportunities in front of you. What do you choose? I can't tell you I have the answer, but what I usually do (that I didn't in the situation I just mentioned but should have) is pray about it, seek wise counsel if I have the time, and make a decision.

One of my best qualities can work against me sometimes, and I wonder if you ever have the same problem: sometimes I can be a people pleaser. I want to make people happy. I want them to be proud of me. If I can make a difference in someone's life, I'm in!

Do you know what the last person in line for whom I'm able to sign an autograph or take a selfie is feeling? Pretty pumped and excited. You know what the people behind them are thinking? That I'm a pretty crummy guy because I didn't get to sign something for them.

While I know that I screw up all the time, I still strive to live by my convictions. For Demi, I strive to love her in a sacrificial way and grow better, each day, at being the husband she deserves. Feelings fade and change like seasons, but when you base your actions, your attitude, your decisions, and your behaviors on your convictions, most of the time you can expect a positive outcome. But there's one conviction that will never disappoint us, even when life doesn't turn out the way we had planned or expected.

Holy Confidence

As believers, our convictions must rest in our identity in God and in who He is. The Bible tells us that "Jesus Christ is the same yesterday and today, and forever" (Hebrews 13:8). In every season and in every circumstance, we can trust God's character! Scripture gives us a thorough picture of His very nature. God is holy,[4] righteous,[5] just,[6] merciful,[7] loving,[8] kind,[9] faithful,[10] gracious,[11] compassionate,[12] good,[13] and wise,[14] to name a few attributes. God loved us so much that He severed a perfect relationship with His Son so we could be made right with Him. He gave up His child for you and for me. I don't know about you, but that's someone I can trust.

We may wrestle with not knowing or liking the plans God has for us. We may nurse disappointment because of the detour our career path or relationship took. We may feel like a failure because the work we do isn't posted and seen by many on social media. And we may have to find healthful ways to work through those feelings. But in those moments, by choosing to cast our cares on Jesus, we are choosing to trust in the character of God. We may not know or understand what God is doing or where He is taking us, but we can take to heart His words:

My thoughts are not your thoughts,
Nor are your ways My ways. . . .
For as the heavens are higher than the earth,
So are My ways higher than your ways
And My thoughts than your thoughts.
  (Isaiah 55:8–9)

God has given us His best, His Son, and has proved that He can be trusted. I may not understand why certain roads have started or ended, but I can count on His faithfulness. I know this sounds so simple—and powerful if lived out—but there are times I fail to remember this truth. It's mind boggling to me. I've been a Christian most of my life, almost three decades, yet I still allow myself to worry about the stupidest things or let my emotions rob me of the best of my days. Cue the scene of me walking around the Cowboys' complex sulking because I'm not playing football. I forget that I can trust God because He gave up His best, His only Son, for me.

And when I remind myself of that truth, those ugly feelings begin to dull.

The Bible tells us that one day Jesus got heart-breaking news. I'll preface this story by saying that John the Baptist was Jesus's cousin. He also played a pivotal role in the Messiah's life: John announced His cousin's arrival to the people of Israel. He also had the privilege of baptizing Jesus. But something bad had happened to John. After he was thrown in jail by King Herod, John was executed at the prompting of the king's daughter (see Matthew 14:6–12). When John's disciples share with Jesus the horrible news, Jesus is crushed. His cousin, His friend, His partner in sharing that "the kingdom of heaven is at hand" (3:2), is dead. When Jesus finds out, He does what most of us would do in this situation: He seeks solitude. He tries to withdraw to a desolate place to be alone. He turns his phone off. He draws the curtains shut. He ignores the knocks at the door. Of course He does. Jesus wants to grieve, by Himself, for someone He loved so much. But He doesn't get to do this immediately.

> **When emotions lead you to consider calling it quits, your convictions will remind you that you can push a little harder or go a little further to reach your goal.**

While attempting to retire to a private location by boat, the crowds catch wind of Jesus's whereabouts and meet Him onshore. When He disembarks the vessel and is greeted by a chatty throng of people, He mutters something unmentionable under His breath. And throwing His hands up toward heaven, He yells, "Can't I have one minute alone, please?" Wait, that's not it. Let's try again: So Jesus takes one look at the crowd and runs in the opposite direction as fast as He can. Hmmm, that's not right either. Instead, He "felt compassion for them and healed their sick" (14:14). Yeah, that sounds much more like Jesus. Instead of remaining alone, He teaches them. He interacts with them. He heals the sick. And in one of the greatest miracles in the Bible, Jesus feeds this crowd of five thousand families with only five loaves of bread and two fish, a lunch given to Him by a little boy (see verses 15–21). I can't imagine Jesus was in the perfect frame of mind to perform miracles that afternoon, yet He lived by His convictions. What an example for us.

Emotions will never be consistent. They may be good, like joy or amusement, but they might also take a darker route, like pride or jealousy. Yet convictions offer consistency. When your convictions are rooted in whose you are and living a mission-possible life, they will drive you toward your calling. When emotions lead you to consider calling it quits, your convictions will remind you that you can push a little harder or go a little further to reach your goal. When your emotions tell you that "good enough" is good enough, your convictions make you realize that you can be better.

We don't know all the things God is doing in us, through us, by us, or around us, but we get to trust that He loves us, because He demonstrated it. We didn't love Him first. He loved us first. And when we live by that conviction, we can rest with a holy confidence that "all things . . . work together for good to those who love God, to those who are called according to His purpose" (Romans 8:28).

8

EMBRACE THE GRIND

It is no use saying, "We are doing our best." You have got to succeed in doing what is necessary.
—WINSTON CHURCHILL

IF THERE IS A PARADISE ON EARTH, IT would have to be the Maldives, where Demi and I honeymooned in the beginning of 2020. Made up of more than a thousand islands, some of which are uninhabitable and nothing more than isolated strips of sand, this country reflects with accuracy the stock photos you see of crystalline beaches and whimsical overwater villas atop turquoise seas that beg you to take a dip. The place where we stayed was situated in the middle of the Indian Ocean and was nothing but miles and miles of fifty breathtaking shades of blue under clear skies. It was as though we were castaways but with all the amenities Tom Hanks only dreamed of having (and minus Wilson).

While I like to think of myself as more of an action guy—I am, after all, the one who arranges snake-wrangling competitions and kayak races on the Tebow family vacations—this was definitely more of a laid-back atmosphere. Lots of snorkeling, swimming, and sunbathing. There were maybe forty or fifty people on the whole island, so it often felt like we were the only ones there.

I think it was on day five that we enjoyed our first-ever stargazing dinner. Our resort offered an observatory that hosts one of the largest overwater telescopes in the Indian Ocean. A few tables surrounded this massive telescope, which was connected to a screen on each table. After we ordered our dinner, the resident astronomer showed us around the galaxies of the northern and southern hemispheres. As he navigated the skies while we gaped in awe in turns through the telescope, I could tell he was passionate about what he did. I remember asking him, "With all your knowledge of the stars and the universe, would you say that you believe more or less in God?" He shrugged and shook his head. "I don't believe in God," he stated matter-of-factly. I didn't want to force a conversation he didn't want to have, so we continued our tour of the skies.

When our dinner arrived, Demi and I traded the telescopic view of the skies to savor each bite of our mouthwatering cuisine. I don't know what smelled better, the refreshing saltwater scent of the open ocean or the robust aroma of filet mignon. As the lagoon's gentle waves lapped around us and with our evening itineraries nowhere in sight, I was the most relaxed I'd ever been. Being completely at rest is really challenging for me. It doesn't come naturally. But tuned into Demi's sweet voice as soft music played in the background, it was easy to focus on this rare time of quiet together.

Suddenly a screech erupted from the communal area of the resort about 150 feet away. It made Demi and I both jump out of our seats. It was followed by an outburst of angry voices. Layers of distressed sounds magnified in the otherwise tranquil space. Instinct took over and I practically hurdled the table and Demi, and took off at high speed to see what the commotion was about.

"Where are you going?" Demi called out through the dust of my hasty exit.

"I have to go check what's wrong!" I yelled back as I raced down the snaking jetty over the lagoon. I assure you, before I took off, I made sure that Demi was absolutely not in any danger at all. I would never do anything to jeopardize my wife's safety, but I knew I had to do something!

As I got closer to the indeterminable scene, I discovered the source of the ruckus.

The scene was a chaotic frenzy. Ten or so adults were screaming at each other in a foreign language, their faces flushed with rage. Half-eaten meals were splattered all over the floor. Broken glass from stemware littered the now filthy table. I had no idea what anyone was saying or what they were fighting about. Some staff tried to help calm tempers, and more arrived on the scene just after I got there. They did a great job of cooling a heated atmosphere.

From what I could gather from speaking to a staff member later, the event was a dinner party made up of two families. What started out as a harmless argument about where COVID-19 originated turned into one family taking deep offense. They felt they had to defend their hometown against a hurled accusation that the disease had begun there.

But this story isn't about a virus or where or how it originated. It's about making each day, each moment, count. It's about saying yes when it matters and being ready when opportunity strikes. It's about being prepared and willing to step up when the occasion arises.

I may not have won the Best Date award that evening when I bolted from our stargazing dinner to check out the problem and see if I could assist, but I would rather choose to help over doing nothing any day.

Even though I was on my honeymoon, that didn't mean the mission-possible part of me was on vacation. It wasn't taking a break and frolicking with the dolphins in the Indian Ocean. I want it to be who I am. If there was a problem, I was going to see if I could help in any way.

Power in the Details

Not every day is game day. Not every day is a day that our foundation rescues human trafficking victims. Not every day is a day we grant a sick child a W15H. Not every day is a day we get to bring a special-needs orphan to his or her new forever family. But every day is a day we get to push the mission forward. This means that every day we are doing research, making phone calls, setting up appointments, having meetings, conducting interviews, creating budgets, finding sponsors, making partnerships, and so much more. You know what a lot of this is? The grind. Putting in the hard, necessary, and daily work that is pretty unglamorous that people on the outside don't get to see and don't realize how much there is or what it takes to get done. The grind can be rote, such as practicing the same shot a million times or confirming reservations for the fourth time, and can seem on the surface to be absent of meaning or reward.

Those moments don't have the payoff, but if you don't put in those moments, you'll never get the payoff. What's just as important as game day is the accumulative value of the practices and training put in on Tuesday morning and Wednesday night and Thursday afternoon. In fact, the tip-off matters more when each day that week you attacked your drills for hours when no one was watching. The writer Alan Armstrong said, "Champions do not become champions when they win the event, but in the hours, weeks, months, and years they spend preparing for it. The victorious performance itself is merely the demonstration of their championship character." This is the mindset of hard work, practice, grit, and endurance—all ingredients that dreams are made of.

> **There is nothing neutral about living a mission-possible life.**

You don't have to be an athlete to engage in life with this kind of intensity; you just have to live mission possible. There is nothing neutral about living a mission-possible life.

I think of our W15H program. Since we started this program in 2011, nearly one hundred children and teenagers with life-threatening illnesses have received an official all-inclusive experience sponsored by our foundation in which they spend a weekend enjoying customized daily activities, gifts, meals, and time with me. (Hundreds of Brighter Day experiences have been provided, which include hospital visits, phone calls, and video chats.) So many weekends come to mind, but I especially remember the one with brothers Andrew, twelve at the time, and Aaron, thirteen. Both brothers were diagnosed with a rare form of brain tumor. Their weekend was a big moment for everyone involved since it was a double W15H. It took place in Atlanta at the 2019 SEC Championship Game, Georgia versus Louisiana State University. We had a great time teasing each other about our rival sports teams.

I also got to spend a weekend with Ben, a kind thirteen-year-old who has cystic fibrosis. Ben and I discussed how God uses our difficult seasons for His glory. We also talked about the importance of our daily routine of eating and exercise and how that makes us better athletes. And I'll never forget the W15H weekend with Josh, a courageous young man from Mississippi who had medulloblastoma. It was an emotional night for all of us in the room, and it was so special to see God working in his life. Though the W15H eventually comes to a close, our relationships with these families do not. They will always be permanent members of the TTF family.

Putting together a W15H weekend is no easy task. The week of the W15H, Kelsey, who heads our program at TTF, resembles a blur as she darts in and out of the office, running up and down the stairs to prepare merch, and is constantly on the phone scheduling and rescheduling, and rescheduling the rescheduled schedules. Here's a glimpse into the process of a W15H so you get an idea of what I'm talking about.

A W15H request comes in and Kelsey touches base with the family and the child. Without promising anything, she finds out what we can do to show their son or daughter our support. She also has to confirm via a doctor's note that the illness or disease is in fact life threatening. (Yes, we've had situations where that was not the case.) And from there, her checklist is about a mile long and includes working with the child and parents to fill out his or her favorite things (color, superhero, sport, movie, hobby, song, book, snack), budgeting the weekend, arranging flights and hotel accommodations, making restaurant reservations, decorating their weekend hotel room with all the child's favorite things, planning special activities, arranging gifts, coordinating arrival and departure for each event on the itinerary, and coordinating logistics with **SEC Nation** or whatever cool event we are part of that weekend. The responsibilities I just mentioned are just a glimpse of the details that are ironed out to make a weekend perfect for a child and his or her family.

Before the pandemic, I didn't know where I would be on the weekend until the Sunday before, and then Kelsey would have four days to arrange all the details. I was traveling so often, especially during baseball season, that there were times I would spring a W15H weekend on her two days before. And although to the human eye that feat seemed close to impossible to accomplish in such a short amount of time, Kelsey would accept the mission with a smile—and get it done. I never saw her sweat, either, but I'm sure she probably did.

Because she had planned in advance (by regularly checking our merch inventory, staying in touch with families, forming relationships with contacts, and researching information even before she needed to), if I told her that, say, I was going to be in Charlotte that next weekend and was wondering if she could find a child there for us to celebrate, she was able to track one down in a moment's notice. Oh, it was still stressful for her, and many times she wondered how on earth she was going to pull it off, but by the grace of God, every W15H weekend exceeded my expectations.

> **There's power in the details.
> There's purpose in being prepared.**

Kelsey attends every W15H weekend to ensure all logistics run smoothly. I'm glad she can be able to witness the fruits of her labor. The look on the face of a child who walks into a hotel room that has been decked out in his or her favorite colors and superhero decor is priceless. Even more so is getting the opportunity to experience the faith, hope, and love these children, who battle life and death every day, share with us. Kelsey says, "We at the foundation often say that although most people think we are blessing the family, any one of us who are there know that we are the ones who walk away so encouraged." It's truly humbling to meet a child who knows the true meaning of suffering and pain and have him or her look into your eyes and tell you with confidence, "God is good. And I believe He can heal me."

There's power in the details.

There's purpose in being prepared.

When you pursue the grind with purpose and truly devote yourself wholly to live mission possible—even on your honeymoon, even the day after the national championship, even when the W15H weekend is over—you continue to prepare yourself for the next moment that comes. And the next, and the one after that.

It's About the End Goal

The grind may not be exciting. Often it sucks. The hours are long and painful, and I've learned that not many people come alongside that side of the journey. It's more fun to show up for the games, the concerts, the rescues, and the galas, but few show up when the blood, sweat, and tears are being ground out. But that's a story for another time.

One person who has lived each day, with joy and grace, in order to fulfill his mission is my dad. His mission is to preach the gospel to every person in the Philippines. I'll never forget how when I was growing up I'd wake up and get breakfast downstairs, and my dad would always be sitting at the table reading his Bible and other study material. I believe his consistency and the passion he's had for his calling and his life over the years has had the most positive influence on me. Decades later, he is still consistent and passionate. He maintains stellar focus and an unmatched energy that could put to shame twenty-year-old men. Despite his older age and his diagnosis of Parkinson's disease, he continues to drive forward with passion and intensity. He doesn't let fatigue stop him. Even as his body is depleted of energy, he presses forward and travels back and forth from the United States to the Philippines to fulfill what God has called him to do. I pray I have the same type of stamina Dad has when I reach his age.

Working hard is not the end goal; we work hard to get to the end goal.

You know why Dad is this way? It's not because he is Superman or was born with extra reserves of energy or intestinal fortitude that most of us weren't naturally blessed with. It's because he invests himself into the mission and works hard at it because he knows the payoff is worth it.

A few weeks ago, I held a staff retreat for my team at the foundation. I thought it would be cool to have Dad come out for the afternoon and field some complex theological questions our staff had been asking. I study really hard to be equipped to lead our team, but I wanted Dad to be there because he has so much to offer in that regard.

Not only was Dad there to answer some really hard questions (which he did for hours and backed up with tremendous amounts of Scripture), but he also helped the team fine-tune their gospel presentations. The gospel is important to us at TTF. In fact, it's the most important message we as Christians will share in our whole lives. First Peter 3:15 tells us, "Always [be] ready to make a defense to everyone who asks you to give an account for the hope that is in you, but with gentleness and respect." After offering some coaching pointers on how to "give an account," Dad ran the team through some practice gospel presentations. He taught with respect, kindness, and patience—even when one of the practice presenters forgot to mention the Resurrection entirely. Dad did an amazing job and shared so much love and wisdom with our team. I could not have been prouder. When I walked him to his car that afternoon, I thanked him from the bottom of my heart. I'll never forget what he told me as we shortly debriefed the meeting: "I stayed up until 4 a.m. studying the book of James."

This is coming from a man who has read the book of James, and the entire Bible for that matter, probably a thousand times. He was so invested in this staff retreat session and the lives of those who would be in attendance that he contributed hours and hours of effort into studying something he'd already studied. And he was more than happy and willing to put in the work to do it.

Let's talk about hard work for a minute. A work ethic is pointless without a purpose. Working hard is not the end goal; we work hard to get to the end goal. I know that not everyone is working their dream job. But the Bible teaches us that even if you dislike what you do or don't feel you fit in at work, "Do your work heartily, as for the Lord and not for people, knowing that it is from the Lord that you will receive the reward of the inheritance. It is the Lord Christ whom you serve" (Colossians 3:23–24). Even if where you are isn't where you want to be, God can still use you.

One of the emptiest things I hear well-meaning teachers, coaches, and even parents say is how proud they are of someone's work ethic. I don't mean to say it's a terrible thing to be proud of, but it's essentially meaningless if there's no purpose beyond self-achievement. Why would you get up at 4 a.m., or work out twice a day, or study most weekends, or do any number of hard things without a good reason? It might seem crazy, but to me that's a waste of time. If you're a believer, your purpose is ultimately to glorify God, right? To love and serve God and others. Discipline, patience, endurance, and work ethic are valuable things in and of themselves, but they have more meaning when they are connected to a higher purpose. Harness discipline and a solid work ethic, and use them as tools to point in the right direction.

My dad is committed to his mission, and he was committed to making the most out of his time with my team. Instead of relying solely on his knowledge and experience, of which he had plenty, he prayed and studied for hours to be prepared to point each person present at that staff retreat to Jesus.

When I think of commitment, I see the face of Brandi, the foundation's vice president of ministries. She's worked with me for more than ten years. Not only do I highly value her as an esteemed member of our team, but I treasure her as a friend and confidante. If TTF had a heart, it would be Brandi. It's because she never turns off. She has embraced the grind with upmost commitment, compassion, and foresight. She's always ten steps ahead, so I never have to worry about a W15H or family we serve coming unglued due to a complication within our control.

One of the many characteristics that make Brandi shine above others is her commitment to both our team and the families we serve. She has taught us through her example of what it means to be a prayer warrior. Camryn, who also works with us, says, "I've sat back and watched her seek the Lord on behalf of people countless times, whether that's those we are considering hiring or our W15H families. I can't tell you how often we were on a W15H together and she'd just stop and say, 'Let's pause and pray.' Brandi has taught me so much about the power of prayer. She is more than a boss; she is a mentor and a friend."

> **Discipline, patience, endurance, and work ethic are valuable things in and of themselves, but they have more meaning when they are connected to a higher purpose.**

Kelsey, whom I previously mentioned in this chapter, often brags about Brandi's deep sense of loyalty. "She knows how to love well, and she has counted the cost of what that will take. She will not hesitate to rearrange her entire schedule to hop on a plane to the other side of the country to help someone who is sick or in need. Brandi has shown me what it means to go above and beyond in serving others."

There is No <u>Yet</u>

Name something you are committed to. Your marriage? Your family? A sport? A product you sponsor? Your job? The book or song you're writing? It's so easy to be hyped up and fully engaged in a project or person in the beginning. It's new and exciting. All the happy hormones like oxytocin, dopamine, and serotonin are flying high. You're running on so much adrenaline that you don't need much sleep. But a few months down the road—when these natural chemicals wear off and you realize that the person you have fallen in love with has quirks you're not excited about, or the book or song you've been working on is on its ninth draft and it's still not quite right—calling it quits sounds appealing. It's too hard, right? It's requiring too much work! **This isn't what I signed up for!**

For some of you, this might sound like something that comes to mind in moments of challenge or difficulty in marriage. Remember the vows you exchanged while gazing lovingly into one another's eyes? "For better, for worse, for richer, for poorer, in sickness and in health, to love and cherish, until death do us part." When you recite those powerful lines while dressed to the nines with all your friends and family cheering you on, they seem to roll off your tongue.

But what happens when the worse comes before the better? Or before the seemingly "worser"?

Jeff and Becky Davidson got married in 1991. Jeff knew after only two weeks of them dating that Becky was the one, and the couple got engaged three months later. They had both scripted the stories of the rest of their lives as individuals and as a family. Jeff would continue to climb the corporate ladder. Becky was going to teach school for a while. Then, when the time was right, she would stay home to raise their children in their big house in the suburbs. They quickly realized they had much less control over their stories than they had thought. Becky's first pregnancy ended in a miscarriage. Their son, Jon Alex, was born in September 1997. The couple was delighted and hoped their perfect plan was finally set in motion. As months passed and Jon Alex didn't reach certain milestones, their worries carried over into a diagnosis they weren't prepared for. One doctor's visit led to multiple others. It was discovered that Jon Alex had cerebral palsy, autism, and epileptic seizures and would be nonverbal. Unable to walk, talk, or function independently, he would require profound round-the-clock care for the rest of his life.

Though Jeff and Becky battled questions and anger at first, they ultimately settled into a space of trusting God. In Jeff's words,

> The world looks at my son and sees a nonverbal young man crippled by cerebral palsy, intellectually disabled, and profoundly affected by autism. The world sees a boy who can't walk, talk, or function independently.
> I don't see that. I see a beautiful masterpiece.
> I see a tapestry of God's grace, God's beauty, and God's love woven together in a humble child. The world sees paint on damp plaster. I see the ceiling of the Sistine Chapel. The world sees a broken boy. I see Michelangelo's **David.**"[1]

Becky said this: "Jeff and I came to a place of acceptance and believed deep in our souls that our son was wonderfully made and created for a plan and purpose. Instead of allowing the hardships and trials we faced to tear us apart, we purposed in our hearts to allow them to draw us closer together."

In 2005, the Davidsons started a ministry called Rising Above, a multidimensional outreach organization to special-needs families. They appointed Jon Alex as the CIO, Chief Inspirational Officer. Jeff and Becky never would have imagined the work they were able to accomplish in helping other families with children with special needs. From a small local outreach providing faith-based support groups, weekly Bible studies, and regular family outings and activities, Rising Above has grown to a national level, helping sponsor monthly events and activities and even a small-group curriculum used around the world.

Things were starting to look up. But in 2009, Jeff got sick. What began as a chronic foot problem over the years required a leg amputation and turned into renal failure with chronic kidney disease. For years, Jeff was in and out of the hospital more times than Becky can remember. He had more surgeries than she can count. He had coded and was in the ICU on a ventilator so often that it seemed more common than not. For a time, both Jeff and Jon Alex used wheelchairs. It was quite a feat for Becky to maneuver the two of them around on her own. From 2015 through 2017, Jeff was unable to care for himself, and Becky became his caregiver while continuing to remain Jon Alex's. I want to share a few thoughts Jeff penned in a blog post, in which he painted a powerful picture of how he saw Becky fulfilling her roles as a committed parent and spouse in a time of crisis:

She sits quietly in the chair beside his hospital bed.

The same chair where she has sat all night long for the past week while her husband lies in the hospital. . . .

She is beyond weary. . . . For the past week she has desperately balanced having her husband in the hospital with the demands of also being the mother of a child with profound special needs.

She alternates her time between the hospital and home where her family is assisting with the care of her son. To say she is sleep deprived would be a huge understatement. . . .

This is not the life she expected or dreamed of when they got married all those years ago. She never imagined she would raise a son who requires 24/7 care with his every need. And then to have a husband struck by a chronic illness in midlife. It is overwhelming at times. . . .

Compassion fatigue is real and it's emotionally crippling. She wants to cry but there's no time to really process what all is going on in her life.

The social worker from the hospital slips into the room to discuss his care when they leave the hospital. "Who will take care of him when you return home?"

Quietly she chuckles and says, "I will. We've been married for twenty-five years and I'm not going anywhere."

The social worker turns to her and says, "Yet."

In a voice that leaves no doubt or equivocation, she turns to the social worker and says, "There is no 'yet.'"

Twenty-five years. Sickness and health. Better or worse.

Because we took a vow. A covenant before God. A promise that didn't include the word "yet." . . .

The toil it takes on your marriage is staggering. Then throw in a spouse living daily with a chronic illness. It's intense and even brutal. But we had taken a vow.

Right now, there are many of you ready to check out. You feel like you've reached your breaking point in your marriage. You're ready to walk out the door on your marriage any minute.

For all of you in the midst of the struggle . . . for all the special needs moms and dads about to throw in the towel and quit . . . for all of you ready to just give up and walk away . . . for all of you wondering if it ever gets better . . . for all of you struggling to find anything good about your circumstances . . .

There is no "yet."[2]

I met the Davidson family the week of Night to Shine in 2016 on one of our stops in Cookeville, Tennessee. A friendship blossomed immediately. Jeff and Becky opened my eyes to just how hard it is for parents who have a child with special needs. That day I became a better person just for having met the family.

Starting on May 11, 2017, and continuing for thirteen days, Jon Alex and Jeff were admitted on several different occasions to separate hospitals. Becky says it was the most overwhelming time she's ever experienced in her life.

During those thirteen days, Jon Alex suffered from the flu and severe dehydration and had two seizures, one a grand mal. Jeff was scheduled for emergency surgery on his foot, but he coded shortly after being taken to the operating room, so a pacemaker was installed. Early the next morning, Jeff coded again and was put back on a ventilator in the ICU. At the same time Becky walked into her husband's room, she received a phone call from her sisters who were caring for Jon Alex. He was having a massive seizure, and they had just called 911. Jon Alex was admitted to the hospital later that day.

Becky spent the next morning, May 23, with Jon Alex until after his doctors completed their rounds.

Then it was Jeff's turn. When she arrived at the ICU, suddenly multiple alarms screamed. Her husband was coding for the third time. Although doctors revived Jeff again, they told Becky there wasn't anything else they could do and that it wouldn't be long before it happened again. As hours passed and friends and family gathered around Jeff's bedside, Becky leaned in close to her husband and whispered, "There **was** no yet." Those were the last words she ever spoke to him.

I love what Becky told me: "Had I not done the hard things, had I cut bait and run, I would have more regrets now than I think I could bear. I am able to look back at my life with Jeff and know that even though it was excruciating at times, we both loved each other well and remained committed until the last moment of his life on earth. I am so grateful for that."

Those words were spoken by a woman who truly believed there is no yet. It's an inspiring and wise principle to live by. Becky's story is a telling example of what it looks like to be all in. No excuses. No regrets.

We never give up our mission to love God and others. We never quit serving God and others. We don't quit praying for our loved ones' freedom from addiction, for their salvation, for their healing, for their wholeness. We don't stop studying, practicing, and preparing.

There is no "yet."

Find the Right Balance

When you are committed to a mission, nothing can stop you. You live with a heightened sense of awareness, particularly of your purpose. You have a vision of who you are and who God created you to be. You understand that your time on earth is limited and live with an underlying sense of urgency. You focus on what you need to do now and what you need to do next. When you live with this level of commitment, some might describe you as **intense.**

If you watch, as an outsider, two NFL teams during a practice, you'll probably think both teams are working super hard. And you're probably right. But as an insider, you can see their work ethic on a much deeper level. You'll be able to tell the difference between the players who are practicing with an "I'm working hard and I'll probably be sore tomorrow" attitude versus an "I'm working hard and I'll probably not be able to move in the morning" attitude. The latter is the kind of intensity that makes a difference on and off the field.

Picture a boardroom. The presenter holding the meeting is locked into the topic at hand, unaffected and unperturbed by the room temperature, the lack of snacks on the table, the horrible artwork on the wall, or the stain on the shirt of the guy in front of him or her. Coaches Urban Meyer and Bill Belichick were the best at locking in with this kind of focus and intensity. It's not enough to just practice; you have to do your best at each practice. It's not enough to show up for a meeting; you've got to be homed in during the entire hour. It's not enough to wake up and get out of bed; you have to live with open eyes to see the needs, an open heart to love, and open hands to serve.

I want to inspire people to have that kind of intensity.

I was born a very intense guy. I'm rather competitive by nature. I rarely take downtime. I'm not saying it's not important, but I just don't do it much. Rest is good. God rested on the seventh day of the creation. Rest is biblical. But one of my worst qualities is not stopping and resting and pausing. I'm getting better at it, though. (At least I think I am—maybe I'll have to ask Demi.) Taking time off is definitely a challenge because I feel the weight of hurting people around the world. In my mind, if I take a vacation or watch a movie or read a book or do any number of things unplugged, that's one less boy or girl who gets faith, hope, and love. That's one less person who gets to receive a hug or get lavished with love or get cared for. That kind of pressure weighs heavily on me, and even though I realize it's a weight that's not mine to carry, I struggle to let it go.

I'm working on finding the right balance between pursuing my mission with locked-in intensity and resting enough so I can recover enough to continue fighting with passion.

Most of us struggle with finding balance of some

kind. Some people have no problem resting. They could snooze or read a book or watch movies uninterrupted for hours. Their couch has an indentation of their body to prove it. Others work so hard their loved ones need to pry their fingers off their computers at night.

Balance is a funny word. I don't know if we get it right all the time. I haven't found a formula for that yet. If you've got one, let me know. What I think is most important is to step back, look at the big picture, and pray. What do you want your life to look like? What kind of person do you want be? Like Becky Davidson, I think we all would want to say we have no regrets. We're not meant to live perfect lives, but we were created to live mission-possible ones. And I believe the path of purpose has far fewer regrets.

9

PURPOSE
IN THE WAITING

**God does not give us everything
we want, but he does fulfill his
promises . . . leading us along the
best and straightest paths to himself.**
—DIETRICH BONHOEFFER

A SONG BY TOM PETTY PROCLAIMS,
"The waiting is the hardest part."[1] Just ask anyone
waiting to get chosen for the dream job, to fall in
love, to see the positive sign on a pregnancy test, for
answers to prayer, or for the test results, and I'm sure
he or she will agree. The Bible is full of stories of he-
roes on brutal journeys through the waiting. While
David is waiting to be crowned king of Israel, he is
on the run from a king who wants him dead. Paul
is in prison while waiting to preach the gospel in
another part of the world. Noah is waiting for rain
to come while fielding doubt and dirty looks.

The psalmist wrote, "Wait for the LORD; be strong and let your heart take courage; yes, wait for the LORD" (Psalm 27:14). I've already talked about the times when God may not fully uncover every detail of our mission plans, but what happens when life takes an unexpected turn and what we thought we had prayerfully and carefully mapped out is not only uprooted but obliterated? What happens when we don't have the luxury of time to figure out what's mission possible because every day it's a blessing just to be alive?

I'm going to pull back the curtain and give you a peek into the life of an incredible boy, Ethan Hallmark, and his parents, Rachel and Matt. This chapter is different from the rest. To give the Hallmarks a few pages simply felt underwhelming. It's a story I've felt compelled to share in great length once I started working on it. Before I give you a glimpse into this unbelievable illustration of one of the most courageous boys I've ever met, the most important thing I can tell you is this: don't waste your waiting.

Let me say that again. Don't waste your waiting.

Purpose is always present, even in the waiting.

As you wait for wisdom, an answer to prayer, or even healing, if you allow Him to, God will always position you to be used for His glory. Purpose is always present, even in the waiting.

Nine-year-old Ethan had often complained about stomach pain, but bellyaches here and there were common complaints from children. Ethan's parents didn't think much of it until the trip they took to South Padre Island off the Gulf of Mexico with their two oldest kids, Ethan and their daughter Lauren, age seven, and two nieces. In the middle of the night, Rachel was startled awake by her niece's hands shaking her shoulder. "Ethan's not feeling good!" the teen lamented.

Rachel leaped out of bed and sped to Ethan's room. Her son was curled up in a fetal position. He was asleep but was moaning, his body twisting and turning in pain. Concerned, Rachel called the doctor in the morning and made an appointment for the next day. She and Matt cut their vacation short a day to accommodate the doctor's visit.

Rachel will always remember the ride back home. As soft shades of orange and pink began to emerge from a pale-blue sky, she turned back to look at the children. All four were asleep. Ethan, eyeglasses still perched on his nose, nestled his head on his sister's lap. **What could be wrong?** Rachel wondered. **Maybe he was constipated? Could it be bad gas?** Nothing serious and definitely nothing life threatening entered her mind. She was convinced that whatever minor problem presented could be cured with some meds or a quick procedure.

She turned around in her seat and stared out the window of the truck. The budding presence of daylight invited more vehicles on the road. People driving to work. Going home. Leaving for a trip. Life rolling in continuous motion. But in the truck, in the wake of quiet, all she could do was think in wild circles. Suddenly the nerves in her body began to tingle in paralyzing fear. In her heart, a voice, quiet yet clear, said, **You're about to go through a storm, but I'm going to meet you there.**

Rachel knew it was God. A mysterious foreboding swept over her spirit as she concluded that the source of Ethan's pain was probably something more serious than gas and would likely require surgery. She could not have been prepared for the depth of the storm that would ambush her son and their family for the next four years.

The next day, Rachel took Ethan to their family doctor. He confidently diagnosed chronic constipation and started Ethan on Miralax. The pain worsened. And the Miralax hadn't helped at all. Two or three days later, Ethan was playing baseball in an All-Star game in Arlington, Texas.

His mother remembers not being able to take her eyes off him as he crouched low in center field, legs spread wide. His hands gripped his thighs as he gritted his teeth in what looked like pain. But when the ball came flying toward him, Ethan instinctively sprang up in the air, his arm shooting high. The ball smacked hard into his thick leather glove as he smashed into the fence right behind him. The crowd went wild. Ethan sank to the ground, then slowly peeled himself up. It was the best final-out catch, but the boy couldn't see the celebration. He saw stars, and from what he later told his mother, it felt like an arsenal of knives were piercing into his legs and gut. Instead of celebrating with his cheering coaches and teammates in the dugout, Ethan hobbled off the field and toward his mother. "Take me home," he begged Rachel.

Within forty-eight hours, a doctor's visit, a CT scan, and a biopsy uncovered the source of Ethan's pain. The discovery swung from terrible to worse. What was first thought to be lymphoma with an 80 percent survival rate was in fact confirmed to be one of the most aggressive pediatric cancers and would most likely end up taking Ethan's life.

On June 30, 2010, Ethan was diagnosed with stage IV high-risk-of-relapse unfavorable-histology neuroblastoma. Seen in infants and young children, the cancer rarely occurs in older kids, and at Ethan's age, it's more difficult to treat and the odds of survival are significantly diminished. It was very lightly scattered in his marrow, and a softball-sized tumor sat in his abdomen. Even if Ethan beat it the first time, doctors warned, he had a 50 percent chance of relapse.

Rachel remembers the moment just before Ethan learned the diagnosis. His eyes were fixed on hers, studying them with great care. "It's cancer, isn't it," he said, raising his arms up and plopping them down on the hospital bed with a frustrated exhale. But disappointment wasn't his only response. "Well," Ethan continued after taking a beat, "I have hope. What do I have to do to get rid of it?"

Ethan spent the next year and a half at the oncology clinic or in the hospital. He endured seven rounds of high-dose chemo, a stem-cell transplant, twenty sessions of radiation, three surgeries, thirty-eight blood transfusions, and five rounds of immunotherapy, which was probably the most painful of all the treatments, since it attacks healthy nerve cells.

I was amazed to hear that Ethan, with great intention, shifted his perspective from one of pain to one of purpose. Honestly, if I had been in the same situation, I don't know if I could have done the same. He said,

> Immunotherapy was the worst part of my treatment. The pain was so horrible, especially when it felt like I was on fire. Lots of times, I thought I couldn't keep going because the pain was too much. Then I would think about how they tortured Jesus and crucified Him. I'd tell myself that Jesus suffered so much more than I ever have and He suffered for me. I knew I could finish the treatment.

For Ethan, what was probably worse than the pain from antibody therapy was the loneliness. Being away from his friends and siblings and his dad, who had to maintain his full-time job to support the family, was akin to torture. Playing Wii with his buddies or engaging in a Nerf war with his little siblings (and letting them win, because that's what good big brothers do) were better drugs at times than morphine.

Seven months into that first year of treatment, having lost weight, his hair, and almost all of his hearing in his right ear, he told Rachel, "Mom, you know what my favorite part of the Bible is? It's where it talks about the light conquering the darkness. You know, even the smallest amount of light can beat the darkest darkness. When you told me I had cancer and everyone was so sad, I still had the tiniest bit of hope. I knew that even the smallest amount of hope would get me through this, the same way the light beats out the darkness." This kind of insight can come only from a spiritual warrior.

In the few years prior to Ethan's diagnosis, his parents noticed he had an unquenchable and un-usual thirst for God's Word for a child of his age. Every night before bed, when it was time to choose a bedtime story, Ethan wouldn't ask for **Goodnight Moon** or **Where the Wild Things Are.** He wanted his father to read him the Bible—specifically, the stories of David in the Old Testament. Ethan found a kinship with this would-be king of an-cient Israel. Interestingly enough, the connection was found not when David sits on the throne as a ruler but when he's on the run from his predecessor, King Saul.

Those stories came alive to Ethan and resurrected him with a new source of strength and comfort after he was diagnosed with neuroblastoma. After his initial diagnosis, he would undergo hour-long scans every three months. Matt would read aloud the stories to his son while the machine whirred its diagnostic melodies and the screen just a few feet away would light up like a Christmas tree high-lighting the numerous spots on his body ravaged by the cancer.

When the scans occurred on September 24, 2011, fifteen months after Ethan's initial diagnosis, there was good news—a miracle! Ethan was 100 percent cancer-free! That day, Rachel wrote on her blog,

Matt and I are forever thankful to our Maker not only for defeating Ethan's cancer but, more importantly, for defeating death for us. We don't know the future for Ethan, nor does anyone their own. However, we know that he is a living miracle! Like David, he has fear-lessly charged the battle line from the moment he heard the giant was awaiting him. Ethan has fought with all of his might—overcoming the most daunting treatment, days filled with horror, and nights of indescribable torment. Yet today he is healed.

Despite the miracle, Ethan continued to suffer the aftermath of the aggressive cancer treatment, including nerve pain, nerve damage, sinus issues, and extensive hearing loss from the platinum-laced chemo. And though the news of remission was no doubt positive, the reality of what the future held was less than assuring. Even if Ethan survived frontline therapy, he had to survive the looming odds of relapse, which doctors noted were roughly 50 percent. Not only that, but the treatment he was receiving for the neuroblastoma put him at risk for contracting leukemia or other secondary cancers.

Prowling lions may be hard to picture if you live in a city or even in the suburbs. Other than in **National Geographic,** they're not a creature we typically encounter. Still, try imagining one with me. The golden fur of the lioness blends into the tall bush. Knees bent, she slowly glides closer to the unassuming prey. Her breath silenced by the rushing of a breeze, she presses in closer, saliva dripping in thick droplets from her razor-sharp teeth. The prey she has marked in her sight relaxes his muscles, welcoming the warm weather as he chews on blades of thin grass. In a split second, the repose is shattered. One pounce, and sharp paws dig into tough skin like a dagger slicing through silk. Neuroblastoma is a disease that attacks when you least expect it and particularly, as the Hallmarks have learned, when you have your guard down. Though scans may not show progress of the illness, it's a sneaky predator. It often stalks in cells undetected, waiting to pounce. It might do so in three months. It might in six months. It may bring friends. They stalk. They're always stalking.

Though the Hallmark family maintained unshakable faith, they were also realistic. Rachel says, "I know the giant my son continues to face, fully aware of its nature and desire to take my son's body and multiply within it. For now, we trust in God's understanding and not our own. We trust in His perfect plan for each of us."

Released from the hospital and returning to the clinic only for checkups and every three months for scans, Ethan was ready to trade infusions for schoolbooks and homework. Returning to school post-frontline therapy was difficult. While he was excited, his eyes had seen so much horror. The kids at school were mostly carefree, but Ethan was fresh off the battlefield. His classmates couldn't possibly understand what he had been through. He had watched multiple friends at the hospital suffer and die. And the reality of relapse was always present. Despite these challenges, Ethan's gratitude about life was overwhelming. He couldn't wait to pick up a bat and start playing ball again.

Two weeks after Ethan learned he was in remission, he gave a talk in his school about perseverance and even showed the students the ten-inch scar on his abdomen where doctors removed the tumor. In his speech, he defined **perseverance** as "having a purpose in life in spite of your difficulties, having a goal and never stopping until you achieve that goal." After Ethan explained the intricacies of cancer and its treatment in terms his peers could understand, he began to encourage them in his inimitable way:

In spite of the difficulty of cancer, I had a purpose. My purpose was to never give up. My faith told me that in any circumstance, the light would always beat the darkness. No matter how dark cancer was, the light would always shine through the darkness. Some of you might be facing problems right now, like bullying or not making the sports team. How can you overcome those difficulties? By persevering, by having a purpose. You have to know that you are special and loved, that God loves you.

Ethan celebrated his eleventh birthday on January 23, 2012, in remission. Rachel wrote,

Humility and thankfulness enveloped me as I sent Ethan off to school this morning. A year ago, the nurse was able to coerce Ethan out of bed to get his weight. It took all of his strength to stand on that scale, his chest filled with hanging tubes, his nose battered with a feeding tube, and every last hair on his body gone from the transplant chemo. Tonight, we will have his birthday party with his buddies. No tubes going into his nose, no port, no central line—he will celebrate this birthday without cancer, without the weight of the world on his shoulders. I can't contain my joy, my tears, over the reality he is alive and able to celebrate his eleventh year of life. His gift—the requested backpack-sized Bible, engraved **Ethan Hallmark, Jeremiah 29:11.**

Scans continued to come back clear until March 2012, when Ethan's oncologist confirmed the worst: the neuroblastoma had returned, this time in the hard bone of his right arm, spanning nearly the length of his forearm, and also in the bone in his upper left arm, in addition to a mass near his bladder. At eleven years old, here is what Ethan wrote a few days after the confirmed relapse:

Some people have been telling me it's okay to yell at God over my cancer relapse. They say God can take my anger. I've been thinking that why would I yell at God when He sent His only Son to die for me? Am I upset? Of course! Our God knows my heart, and He knows that I am hurting. Relapsed neuroblastoma is nothing to be happy about. God has healed me once, and I know He will heal me again either way. But why would I be angry at God when He carried me all this way? Instead of being angry at God, I'm praising Him for the many blessings I have. I'm asking Jesus to heal me from my cancer and to give me strength to endure this treatment. I am blessed by getting to meet new friends who are fighting cancer or other diseases. Getting encouraged by them and me encouraging them is a blessing. I look forward to meeting even more new faces as I fight neuroblastoma. I want to share a verse, Psalm 139:8: "If I go up to the heavens, you are there; if I make my bed in the depths, you are there" (NIV). God is going to be with me through this whole difficult journey. He is always there.

There had to be a mistake. A relapse couldn't be possible. Rachel was sure of it as she stared out the kitchen window and saw Ethan, a glowing smile plastered on his face, dodging Airsoft fire. The midday sun hovered over her boy and his friends as they roared like mighty warriors in the backyard. Just by looking at Ethan as he ran with adolescent speed and ease, you'd never think that both of his arms and his abdomen contained a lethal giant committed to terminating his life, one organ, one bone, one nerve at a time. Death by a thousand cuts.

Doctors recommended intense treatment, bordering hopeful results with sobering reality. Achieving and staying in a second remission wouldn't be easy, but there was a chance worth fighting for.

The Hallmarks' motto during this time? REMISSION POSSIBLE. Rachel wrote,

> Matt and I refuse to be in denial over the reality of this disease. We are preparing ourselves and our son for the journey ahead, even if that path isn't the one we desire. However, what we are also admitting is that our God is able to heal. We pray Jesus is glorified through the miraculous healing to come upon Ethan's body. If that healing comes in heaven, then we will still praise Him for who He is.

A few months later, doctors removed five neuroblastoma tumors.

"How quickly will the tumors grow back?" Rachel asked the oncologist.

"Rapidly," the doctor responded.

On May 16, 2012, Ethan was scheduled for a PET scan. In order for him to undergo one of the more tolerable but aggressive forms of treatment (MIBG radiation), the scan would have to show no growth of any tumors in his abdomen. If it wasn't clear, not only would MIBG treatment not be an option but he would have run out of options.

Rachel sat down with him. "If something bad showed up on the scans, Ethan, would you be okay?"

"You mean am I afraid to die?"

Rachel forced her swelling tears to freeze. Without saying a word, she nodded.

"I'm not afraid to die," Ethan began, "because in the big picture, we are all going to die. I might be eleven and another person one hundred. It doesn't matter. We will all die someday. I don't want to die at an early age. Who does? But I am not afraid to die because I get to spend eternity with God. Some people are afraid to die because they don't know there is eternal life afterwards. Heaven is pure joy, where there is no pain, no suffering, and no evil. I will be in the presence of God and Jesus. As great as we think it is, it will be infinitely better. So why would I be afraid to die?"

With no new growth in his abdomen, Ethan proceeded with the radiation. Two months later, scans showed only a few areas of subtle shading that caused the doctor some concern. Other than those spots, the cancer had been completely eradicated in the abdomen and upper left arm. While the odds two years ago had called for Matt and Rachel to have buried their son by this point, he was alive and well, playing laser tag with his friends. Ethan would continue radiation treatment, stem-cell infusions, and likely indefinite chemo.

"Some people are afraid to die
because they don't know there is
eternal life afterwards. I will be in
the presence of God and Jesus.
So why would I be afraid to die?"

I met Ethan, his parents, and his grandfather on September 16, 2012, while I was playing an away game in Pittsburgh for the New York Jets. The boy made a tremendous impact on me and everyone he met mainly because of his sweet spirit and love for Jesus. I'll never forget how before the game he asked if he could pray for me. His faith was unshakable. After the game, we spent so much time chatting in the locker room that I was late in catching the bus back home. I couldn't help it! I didn't want my conversation with Ethan to end.

Knowing the war was far from over and understanding how aggressive relapsed neuroblastoma is and that it requires indefinite treatment even if remission is achieved, the Hallmarks received a great report a little more than a week after I met with Ethan. All his scans came back clear. Ethan's second remission from cancer was confirmed. He said this about the news:

Thank you for all your continued prayers. God has answered them. Please continue to pray that the cancer never comes back and that I stay in remission. I am so thankful for the healing that God has done in my life. God is so good. God has brought me to the point that science said I wouldn't get to. I am dependent on Jesus, and I'm prepared for whatever life throws at me. Cancer may knock me down at times, but God is the ultimate builder. None of us knows what the future holds, but in all things we know God has special plans for every one of us. We know that if we have faith, we have eternity with our heavenly Father. It is always a win-win situation for those who believe in God.

The year 2012 ended with regularly scheduled scans for Ethan. Halfway through the one-hour MIBG scan on December 29, the tech told him they had to switch to a higher-quality imaging machine that had just opened up. As he slid Ethan out from under the giant capsule, Ethan grinned mischievously and asked the technician, "Can I look at the images you got already?" For reasons Rachel will never know or understand, the tech said yes, and what Ethan saw brought him deep grief.

Rachel remembers sitting in the waiting room next door. From the corner of her eye, she noticed the door heave open and watched in horror as her emaciated son burst through the door and collapsed right into her lap. Ethan's body quaked in violent sobs of anguish. Tears surged from his bloodshot eyes. He was convinced both of his arms had lit up on the screen, showing signs of the disease. The tech assured Rachel the images her son saw, that he obviously should not have been privy to, were crude and imperceptible to a child.

Rachel said this: "I tried desperately to console a boy who had every right to deeply grieve. I wanted to believe he was mistaken, but my heart knew he was right. He is too bright, too experienced in the world of suffering." The scans confirmed the cancer had returned in both arms and also a new spot on his vertebrae. Having to tell Ethan the news was one of the hardest things Rachel had to do.

He knew before a word fell out of my mouth. Unable to even speak, I just pointed to his arms, to the places that held the disease. Nothing I said from that point on could console my sobbing son. He didn't scream or cry out loud—just gentle, soft sobs. No bitterness or anger has come from him; he just doesn't want to have to face the giant again. He knows full well the power of the giant that laughs at him. He knows his situation is very grim. Ethan let me immediately know he is fighting this beast with all he has, but he also made it clear his heart is in excruciating pain like it has never felt before. Sitting there in that recovery area, I talked to my son

about life and death. How many conversa-
tions on this must I have with this child?

As tearstained mother and son had a conversation
that would continue to cycle through their time
on earth together, Ethan told his mother, "I'm not
afraid; I just don't want to do this again."
Rachel swallowed hard. She hated what she
was about to say but knew she had to say it. "It's
your body, Ethan. You have a say. You get to make
this choice."
"No, Mom. I don't mean that. I don't want to
have to fight this again, but I will. I'm fighting," he
said. His voice was firm as his eyes welled with tears.
The Hallmarks opted to assail the neuroblastoma
with aggression. In addition to chemo and blasting
both arms with radiation, doctors opted to radiate
the collarbone as well. If the disease was there prior
to the radiation, it was assumed it would come back.
Ethan was sickened at the news but gripped his faith
tighter. He wrote in his journal,

I've relapsed for a second time. Although
these results were heartbreaking for me, I
am hopeful that God will perform another
miracle. I feel like I had only a short break
from this disease, just like when David was
chased by Saul. As soon as Saul died, David's
own sons started chasing after him. Even
though I am being chased endlessly by this

disease, God is right beside me through it all. Running this marathon is not easy, but I focus on the goal of eternal life. God loved David, but David still endured trials of many kinds. God was always there for David, and He is always there for me. Even though I have cancer, God will not abandon or forsake me. No matter what happens, this disease cannot separate me from the love of God.

The disease stabilized for the next few months as Ethan continued high-dose chemo, radiation, and a new twenty-one-day dose of a trial drug called Fenretinide. Ethan began complaining of a sore throat, and on June 14, 2013, doctors discovered the culprit: a neuroblastoma-filled lymph node in his neck. The mass sat next to a jugular vein and his esophagus. Surgery was successful in removing the mass, as well as twenty-seven neighboring nodes, and more treatment followed. At that point, Ethan's body showed no signs of the disease, but the battle was far from over in keeping it that way. Rachel wrote in her journal,

On June 30, 2010, I wasn't even sure if my son would be alive in a year. Three years later and we're still in a dark valley, deep in the midst of a raging war. Even if my son is blessed with clear scans in a few weeks, there is no end in sight to his therapy. For him to stay alive, his life will be one lived in a permanent war. Grief, pain, and heartache have indeed marked our journey, but so have love, faithfulness, mercy, and compassion.

The scans showed new spots within Ethan's abdominal cavity and spine, buried inside a big muscle that attached to his backbone. Another surgery to remove the soft tissue was scheduled. Shaken but not struck down, Rachel wrote, "Continually, we endure sorrow upon sorrow. My heart is groaning in agony, but I know we serve a mighty, merciful Lord. The glory to come is simply far greater than this insidious disease."

Stabilized, Ethan was put on another clinical trial and sent back to school. He attended football games with his buddies, and the Hallmarks were finally able to have dinner as a family every night, something they hadn't done regularly since Ethan's diagnosis. The neuroblastoma crept closer, its presence greater, showing up as small masses on scans: another on his right knee bone, a spot in his upper left femur, and cancerous lymph nodes on each side of his pelvis. The disease was a slow stalker, but it wasn't stopping.

Rachel wrote,

We've had a few discussions with Ethan's doctor over the past week. From the complexity of his disease to the just-as-complicated therapies, we've covered all ground in our desperate attempts to save our son. Matt and I listened as his doctor confirmed the worst part of all of this: that our son will greatly suffer whether he lives or dies. Knowing there is no end in sight to his suffering, I at times find functioning a difficult task. As a mother, I not only long with every ounce of me for my son to live, but I also long for him not to suffer. The fact this affliction continues to relentlessly abuse him fills my heart with consuming agony every second of every God-given day. As Job said, "What I feared has come upon me; what I dreaded has happened to me. I have no peace, no quietness; I have no rest, but only turmoil" (Job 3:25–26, NIV).

Scans on October 17, 2013, showed a new nickel-sized mass behind Ethan's heart. He began a new trial drug with optimistic faith, feeling a sense of pride as he swallowed eight horse pills in one large gulp. Months later, the mass grew to the size of an egg. Although the cancer progressed at a slow rate and Ethan would start new antibody and chemo treatments, more painful than others, the sleeping giant would never leave. Treatment would stall momentum in one area, and another area would show suspicious activity. Neuroblastoma multiplies uncontrollably, without mercy or regard.

June 30, 2014, marked four years since Ethan was first diagnosed with neuroblastoma. While scans showed the radiation was attacking the cancer, it also showed areas of new growth. In one of the many conversations Rachel had with her son about the gravity of the disease, she asked him if he truly understood that outside of God's miraculous intervention, neuroblastoma is incurable. Ethan responded, calmly and with confidence, "I know cancer is starting to take over my body. I know my body is broken. I hoped God would give me more time on earth, but I'm not afraid of dying or losing my life. I'm just really sad for you and Dad. I don't want you both to hurt like this." Rachel remembers thinking how different Ethan's nature was from the nature of the disease within him. "Loving, compassionate, considerate, and giving, Ethan simply made the world a better place."

While Ethan waited to beat cancer, he used the darkness—what the Enemy meant to destroy him— to bring others closer to the light of Christ.

On a Tuesday morning in the beginning of September, Rachel woke Ethan up to go to the clinic. She immediately noticed distension in his lower abdomen. It made no sense. He hadn't eaten anything in the past two weeks. When the number on the scale at the clinic indicated a considerable gain, a wave of searing pain pierced her heart. **How could he have gained weight without eating?** The findings were devastating. Ethan's abdomen had exploded with hundreds of tumors, too many for the radiologist to even count. They sat on top of his liver, pressed into his ureter, and attached to multiple parts of his intestines. All talk of continued treatment ceased that morning. Ethan was put on hospice care.

Instead of stories about David, Ethan asked his father to read him stories in the Bible about heaven. Six days before his body would finally be rid of the disease and he would meet Jesus face to face, Ethan said this to his parents:

> My biggest fear isn't dying. My biggest fear is that others will blame God for my death and not believe in Him. I don't want people angry at God or even blaming Him. I mean, there is so much more than only this life. Just because He didn't heal me on earth doesn't mean He won't heal me in heaven.

As Ethan grew weaker and his stomach expanded from the multiplying tumors, his friends trickled in and out of the house to say their final goodbyes. They'd sit together on the couch and watch football. They'd make jokes and Ethan's eyes would spark. They'd sit in silence, comfortable in each other's presence without the weight of words. They exchanged final I-love-yous.

In one of Ethan's last days, as he continued to drift in and out of sleep, mumbling incoherently, out of nowhere his voice sharpened. With marked boldness, he stated loudly, "Hi, my name is Ethan Hallmark, and I have been fighting cancer for four years." Through falling tears, his mother whispered into his ear, "Ethan, you fought with bravery and courage. You won. You beat cancer." With his eyes closed, the boy smiled. And on September 26, 2014, Ethan fell into the arms of Jesus. He was welcomed home and was finally made whole.

When Ethan was four years old, Rachel told her husband, Matt, she had a feeling their oldest son would grow up to be a pastor. And, in a sense, he did. Once he was diagnosed, Ethan saw and accepted, with grace and hope, his mission of sharing the gospel through his suffering. Over a third of his life was spent in the trenches of cancer as he faced endless rounds of high-dose chemo, stem-cell transplants, multiple surgeries, more than one hundred days of radiation, and endless travel for trial after trial. On the surface, his life was marked by suffering, but that was only part of the fight. Ethan wanted people to know the truth that the glory to come, the glory found in the priceless gift of Jesus Christ, far surpassed any amount of suffering endured in this temporary world: "I wouldn't trade my relationship with Jesus for anything . . . nothing at all." Ethan wanted a life that represented the size of the prize at the end of this life on earth.

Three months before Ethan passed into heaven, he was gifted with a week at a family camp in Colorado. Every morning a counselor set aside time to talk with him and two other teen boys. One day, this counselor and the three boys discussed what gifts they felt God had given them. Perhaps they were good at serving others or were compassionate. When it was Ethan's turn, he was quick to answer. "My gift is cancer."

Ethan never wanted to die. He didn't enjoy the suffering his gift brought him. He didn't experience joy when his body was pumped with radiation or his nerves were on fire or his mouth was full of so many sores he could barely eat or when he had lost his hearing. But Ethan recognized he could use his gift to reach others for Christ. And every single day, whether he was in agony or given a slight reprieve during remission, Ethan did just that. He did it by how he chose to handle and view his suffering. He did it by encouraging his family, his friends, fellow cancer warriors, and strangers he may one day meet again. Ethan's parents received countless phone calls, emails, and letters from people, young and old, who shared how Ethan's life influenced their own. Some were so inspired by his story of unshakable faith in the face of death that they made the decision to trust in or rededicate their lives to Jesus.

Because God is always in the present, it's always possible to matter, to have meaning, and to make it count—right now.

While Ethan waited to beat cancer, he used the darkness—what the Enemy meant to destroy him—to bring others closer to the light of Christ.

Ethan, mission accomplished!

How was this young man, only nine years old at the time of diagnosis and barely a teenager by the time he crossed over into heaven, able to say that cancer was his gift? How could he keep such a grounded perspective of his identity in Jesus while his body suffered in unimaginable ways? How did he maintain a consistent posture of gratitude during the last few years of his life while he ping-ponged back and forth between miracles and devastating news? Ethan knew God was in control, so he could trust God in the waiting.

I don't know what you are waiting for, but I promise you there is always purpose in the waiting. You may think your life will start when you find your spouse, when you get into that school, when you get picked up by that team, or when you get the job you've wanted since you were a kid. Purpose doesn't show up when that thing finally comes to pass because it might and it might not. Yet because God is always in the present, it's always possible to matter, to have meaning, and to make it count—right now.

Don't wait for purpose to find you someday. Say yes to what God says is possible for and through you in the present.

YOUR LIFE COUNTS

**I have one life and one chance to
make it count for something.**

—Jimmy Carter

MY BUDDY ETHAN SAID A NUMBER OF
profound things. One of them was, "It doesn't matter if you live to be one or one hundred. What matters is what you did for Christ."

One of my biggest goals is to get to heaven one day and hear God tell me, "Well done, good and faithful servant" (Matthew 25:23, ESV).

The world defines success in many different ways. Maybe it's accumulating a certain number of followers on social media, gaining public recognition for an accomplishment, or crossing off the checklist you created when you graduated from college. I hope you reach your goals and get the gold star or hold the trophy up high. But there's something limiting about success as defined by the world. It's self-oriented. The world is going to tell me that success is about opportunity, fame, and fortune for Tim Tebow. It might say that success is praise and promotion for you. In other words, success is about "me." It's inward seeking. It's ours to hold on to. And, ultimately, that kind of success is not fulfilling. In God's economy, He gives us the opportunity to turn success into significance. We can use what we've been given for others. Success in itself isn't a bad thing. There's never been a day in my life in which I've wanted to lose, whether that's a game or a deal. But I also know that if I allow success to be used in only a self-fulfilling way, I will lack purpose. Significance, however, is about others, loving and serving people. One of the greatest questions you can ask yourself is, **Does my life change other people's lives for the better?**

When you're focused on others—when your priorities are wrapped around the Great Commission, bringing the love of Jesus to hurting people—your life counts for more than a title people will forget or an achievement someone will probably surpass in time. Years ago, I heard it said that one of the greatest tragedies in life is to look back one day and say, "I was successful in things that don't matter." I am writing this chapter so that you live today with tomorrow in mind and so that your end goal is not shaped by who the world says you are but rather is anchored in whose you are. I don't want your end goal to be about praise, promotion, and applause; I want it to be about people, purpose, and passion. I preach all the time about living with significance. I try to live it out. That said, I battle daily with doing so. Living with significance is one of the hardest things to do because it doesn't take much to veer off track. I'm running the race for God, and then all of a sudden one self-serving thought creeps into my head and then I'm running the race for myself. I'm constantly trying to keep my head and my heart in the right place, where significance is always my priority. It's not easy, but it's worth it.

One of the greatest questions you can ask yourself is, <u>Does my life change other people's lives for the better?</u>

Every single one of us has a chance to make a difference. We have the opportunity, the ability, and the capacity to do something to build the kingdom of God. It's not because we're great or qualified or successful; it's mission possible because we've teamed up with the God of this universe. When we take aim into the future and live lives of significance, anything is possible.

Make the Choice

Before we start dreaming about what's possible, however, we must remind ourselves of something. Even as we lock into significance over success, the results are beyond our control. We are not tasked with figuring out the complexities and intricacies of God's plan. We are not responsible for the outcomes of our prayers. We allow Him to open or close the doors He chooses for us.

We may not hold the power of foresight, but we have the power of choice. We can choose our attitude. We can choose where we deposit our hope. We can choose in what or whom we trust.

Remember Jeneil in chapter 5? She was a volunteer at Night to Shine whose daughter Rhema struggles with autism, apraxia (an incurable condition in which the brain is unable to make and deliver instructions to the body), and the rare and stubborn seizure disorder. For years, Jeneil battled under the weight of Rhema's diagnoses, challenges, and needs. In the span of ten years, her husband, Brandon, was deployed twice to Iraq and once to Kuwait, with each deployment lasting a year or longer. Caring for Rhema and her other daughter fell heavily on Jeneil's shoulders. As she mothered her two daughters as best as she could, she fought anger, bitterness, and depression. **Where is God in all this?** she wondered. **How will I manage? What does the future look like for Rhema**? In the midst of this uncertainty,

Jeneil knew she couldn't continue living pricked by heartbreak. It was just making everything worse.

In a letter she wrote to me, Jeneil said, "Even though I could not see what God was doing, I had to make a choice to believe that He was and is faithful. My daughter's struggles did not go away. Even now she can still have very hard days with overwhelming senses, self-injuring behavior, aggression, and seizures. But God was doing a healing work in our family, and in many ways it had nothing to do with autism."

Before Rhema was born, Jeneil and her husband chose Romans 10:8–9 as their daughter's theme verse. Jeneil has recited it to her every night at bedtime for the past fourteen years: " 'The word is near you, in your mouth and in your heart' (that is, the word of faith that we proclaim); because, if you confess with your mouth that Jesus is Lord and believe in your heart that God raised him from the dead, you will be saved" (ESV).

Because Rhema had apraxia and was nonverbal, it was impossible for her to communicate. Jeneil longed to have a conversation with Rhema—for her daughter to share why she was upset, what she wanted to wear, what her favorite color was, what made her feel a certain way, and what Jeneil could do to make her feel better. There were signs that Rhema understood far more than doctors had led them to believe. For example, her dad used to put red Crystal Light packets in his water bottles. While he was in Kuwait, Jeneil stopped buying them. The next day, on her iPad, Rhema started tapping a picture symbol of tomato juice. She would do that almost daily. She'd never had tomato juice before, but Jeneil quickly bought her a big bottle of it. When Rhema tried it, she grimaced. It was not what she wanted. But day after day, she kept tapping the picture of tomato juice. It wasn't until one year later, when Brandon came home from overseas with his Crystal Light packets, that Jeneil figured it out. Rhema had tapped a picture of tomato juice and eagerly grabbed a packet of the beverage mix and a water bottle. Amazing! Tomato juice was the closest image she could find to what she wanted. That was one sign that convinced Rhema's parents that she had far more understanding than they were led to believe.

In 2015, Rhema began a teaching method called rapid prompting method (RPM). An individual trained in this technique uses an alphabet board or a tablet and, with words or gestures, prompts a person with autism to point to or tap letters, words, and pictures. Pointing was at first a challenge for Rhema because she lacked the motor skills to form her hand into a point, but Jeneil was determined to work with her daughter using this method.

Mother and daughter first studied the book of Exodus. Jeneil would read from this book in the Bible, ask Rhema a question about it, and then

encourage her to point to a choice, like **y-e-s** or **n-o.**
The two read the Bible together, one word at a time.
With each letter spelled out, the Word of God began
to inscribe itself onto their hearts. It was a painfully
slow process. Each word consumed them both, forg-
ing depth and power little by little.

Lectio divina, Latin for sacred or divine read-
ing, is an ancient meditative spiritual practice of
reading the Bible. In this monastic tradition, one
reads Scripture a few verses at a time, intentionally
slowly in order to listen to God and experience His
presence through His Word. In today's culture of
hurry, it's become commonplace to spend time with
God in the morning by gulping down a one-page
devotional, with maybe a Bible verse somewhere
in the text, and moving on with our day, probably
forgetting what we've read by late morning. The
practice of **lectio divina** does not allow such rush.
In a way, Jeneil was practicing this discipline with
her daughter.

I am writing this chapter so that you live today with tomorrow in mind.

In that sacred space of waiting for her daughter's
heart and soul to connect with her brain and body,
Jeneil sensed that Rhema identified with Moses, a
man who battled his insecurities because of a speech

impediment. A man who didn't think he was capable of speaking, let alone leading the nation of Israel out of Egyptian captivity. A man who would rather live a comfortable life than step into the mission God was calling him to fulfill.

Something in Rhema's spirit seemed to be moved when her mother read how Moses argued with God about why he wasn't the man to lead Israel out of Egypt. "I have never been eloquent, neither in the past nor since you have spoken to your servant. I am slow of speech and tongue" (Exodus 4:10, NIV). Moses's protests didn't change God's opinion of the mission; God reminded the stuttering man of His abiding presence.

As Jeneil continued to read through the fourth chapter of Exodus, detailing the excuses Moses presented before suggesting God find someone better qualified for the job, Jeneil asked Rhema, "What did God say to Moses's objections?" and wrote down different choices on a piece of paper.

Rhema paused. She lifted her trembling hand, clenched into a tight fist as one finger extended beyond the others in a beautiful, hard-won point. She pressed down on the words **I will be with you.** They may not have been audible words, but Rhema understood the question. Even though her brain may have hindered her speech capability, her comprehension was on point.

After a full year of studying with her mother every

night, Rhema spelled her first sentence of open com-
munication. They'd been studying a lesson on the
Lord's Prayer. Jeneil asked her daughter, "What did
you pray for?"

As her mother held up the stencil board, Rhema
pointed to and spelled, "I h-a-v-e m-y v-o-i-c-e."

Jeneil's heart raced. **Could it be true? Had she
imagined what had just happened?** "Can you do
that again, Rhema? Can you tell me again what you
prayed for?"

Once again, "I h-a-v-e m-y v-o-i-c-e."

Jeneil couldn't believe what she was seeing:

It was the most incredible moment of my life
because I knew that God had done it. And
the moment she spelled that she prayed to
have her voice, she had her voice. God an-
swered her prayer then and there. God is
indeed with her mouth and He has given
her a beautiful voice. Like Zechariah whose
tongue was loosed [see Luke 1:64], she is full
of praise and thanksgiving to Him. . . . Once
upon a time, I would have given anything
just to hear her thoughts. Now her words,
in abundance, fill our hearts. In all the si-
lent years, it seemed like God was silent.
But all along He was, and is, speaking. Our
God is a God with perfect plans. He sees and
hears and knows us. He comes down to

deliver us. He teaches us what to say. He performs wonders in our midst. And He is with us.

Two years after beginning RPM, Rhema wrote these beautiful words:

How I love Jesus.
   I am so happy He saved me.
   I was not so happy all the time. My hope was gone, and I was full of despair. I could not speak and no one believed I understood anything. It was so frustrating to not be able to tell anyone how I felt. . . . It was a very painful time in my life. No one could help me.
   Only Jesus knew the loneliness inside my heart. Only He heard the prayers that I prayed. Only He comforted me. He told me that He would one day give me a voice bigger than I could imagine. . . .
   In my silence He showed me how to listen.
   I enjoyed being in His presence. He gave me the ability to hear songs on the trees and music in numbers. My heart filled with gratitude that God would let me hear this beautiful music. One day all of creation will worship the Creator again. I think it will sound like the beautiful music that I hear. . . .
   I think having autism might make some

think I have a sad life. That is not true. I am happy that I am fearfully and wonderfully made. I am thankful for my autism because it teaches me to trust God. My body is not something I can trust but the God who made me is. He not only made me autistic; He made me not able to speak with my mouth but with my heart.

Can you love God when your body betrays you every day? You can.

So much of my trouble with my motor skills comes from sensory overload. It makes me want to jump out of my skin. It is mostly awful to feel this way, but I know the Lord made my body.

So I even will trust Him in this good and mostly mean body.

My hope is in the Lord. I thank Him. For He is always good.[1]

Jeneil made the best choices she could make in one of the hardest times in her life: She chose to fix her eyes on Jesus. She chose to be all in, mothering her children and helping Rhema find her voice. And Rhema? Well, even though the world may look at her as the least and the last, she trusted that the Creator had fearfully and wonderfully made her body.

We, too, have the power to choose. We can choose purpose over our preferences. We can choose to look at our disadvantages as opportunities. We can choose, like Ethan, to fight our battles on this earth with faith in Jesus Christ. And through the sequence of choices we make, we see the hand of providence cover our wounds, our scars, our flaws, our questions, our waiting, our doubts, and our pain with goodness, with grace, and with purpose. "God is able to make all grace overflow to you, so that, always having all sufficiency in everything, you may have an abundance for every good deed" (2 Corinthians 9:8).

> **And through the choices we make, we see the hand of providence cover our wounds, scars, flaws, questions, waiting, doubts, and pain with goodness, grace, and purpose.**

Will you make the choice to begin to see what's mission possible when you trust in Jesus? When you make the choice to say yes, you will change a life. One or many. It doesn't matter—that's up to God.

The choices we make today will have an impact tomorrow. Whether it's how we spend our time, care for our bodies, or treat other people, choices that seem so small can have great significance. Our decisions can give others the courage or the encouragement they need to do something they had never planned on or even imagined they would do.

Be the Reason

In 2020, we at TTF helped sponsor our first Night to Shine in Paris, hosted by the Jérôme Lejeune Foundation. The French capital, nicknamed the City of Lights, the City of Love, and a bunch of other monikers that capture its breathtaking splendor, is nothing short of beautiful. Demi and I marveled at the city's magnificent views, its labyrinth of cobblestone streets, and of course the Eiffel Tower, which bursts with golden sparkles of lights for a few minutes at the beginning of every hour from sundown to 1 a.m. But all that magical wonder would pale in comparison to the beauty I would witness from a young woman later that evening.

As Night to Shine guests began their celebratory jaunt down a red carpet swarmed with cheering people lining the edges, I noticed a girl in a wheelchair being rolled down. Dressed in all black, she wore a red baseball cap that covered the crown of her beautiful tight curls. As she sat in the wheelchair, a smile swelled from cheek to cheek. Her rigid hands met each other in a spastic, awkward rhythm, over and over, the entire length of the red carpet as she squealed in utter delight at the crowd who celebrated her with shouts and applause.

Fifteen minutes later, this young lady was back—this time without a wheelchair. No, she wasn't healed. Her ability to walk didn't change, but she seemed to be so motivated by the cheering volunteers that she had to at least try. With the help of a volunteer, she made her second entrance walking down the red carpet. The beautiful scene brought tears to my eyes. I wasn't sure what disability she had, but she obviously had a hard time walking. She'd swing one stiff leg up in the air (parallel to the floor), stomp it down on the ground, and do the same thing with the next leg, kind of like a soldier's march. As she marched forward with confidence, her warm smile illuminated as much radiance as, if not more than, the glowing Eiffel Tower.

When I think about that young woman, I can still picture her glowing face, her head bobbing up and down with glee as her smile curled up into her eyes. She seemed astonished as she drenched the attention lavished on her. It's a sentiment I've seen in many Night to Shine guests over the years. They can't process how loved and celebrated they are even for one night. It's overwhelming for some. And I like to think that for a few short minutes this woman felt so cherished and so encouraged that she decided to try to walk. She may have needed help. It may not have looked like the type of walking many of us are used to seeing. But as this woman raised one stiff leg up and then another, she seemed to gain more confidence with every step. And if it was even possible, her smile swelled further, drowning her face in the purest kind of joy. I had just spent an incredible day in a breathtaking city with my gorgeous wife (Babe,

I love you so much!), but what shone the brightest that day was the woman who walked down that red carpet.

Watching her made me think of something: I want to be the reason that people think they **can.** I want to be the reason that people have a brighter day. I want to be the reason that people get closer to Jesus. I hope you do too.

What's inside of you that gives you the reason others will believe they can? Success? Maybe. Definitely significance. But even more than that, if you are a believer, it's Jesus. And because of Jesus, namely His death and resurrection, we have the hope and glory of living not for the temporary but for what's eternal.

Infinite Perspective

To live for the eternal is to do things a little differently. Living mission possible means living with an eternal mindset, knowing that our work on earth is to accomplish something of eternal value.

Paul knew this. He wrote, "I have fought the good fight, I have finished the course, I have kept the faith; in the future there is reserved for me the crown of righteousness, which the Lord, the righteous Judge, will award to me on that day; and not only to me, but also to all who have loved His appearing" (2 Timothy 4:7–8).

> **What matters more than the fun we have or the stuff we accumulate is what we did with the time we were given.**

If we live for the here and now, of course we're going to focus on success and fun and living our best lives now. Why wouldn't we want to do whatever we want when we want and how we want to do it? But, as the Bible tells us, this isn't our home.

> Our citizenship is in heaven, from which we also eagerly wait for a Savior, the Lord Jesus Christ; who will transform the body of our lowly condition into conformity with His glorious body, by the exertion of the power that He has even to subject all things to Himself. (Philippians 3:20–21)

We can't get too comfortable with life on earth. We won't be here forever. What matters more than the fun we have or the stuff we accumulate is what we did with the time we were given. The Bible tells us, "If you have been raised with Christ, keep seeking the things that are above, where Christ is, seated at the right hand of God. Set your minds on the things that are above, not on the things that are on earth" (Colossians 3:1–2).

Instead of seeking success in our own lives, we

seek to bring faith, hope, and love to those needing a brighter day in their darkest hour of need. That's not just our foundation's mission statement; that's our hearts' cry. I don't know what your mission is, but I hope it's one that makes your heart long for Jesus and love people.

As children of God, we not only get to live forever with Jesus, but we get to share that hope and that light with others so they, too, can live each day focused on the eternal.

Did you know you were made for eternity? Did you know that this is not your home? My hope and prayer for you is that you are able to say that heaven is your forever home. Jesus came to this earth to bring you good news of great joy. He died for you with eternity in mind. With Him, we can have an abundant life on earth. In riches and power? Maybe. In meaning and significance? Absolutely!

We may not be blessed with Tom Cruise's stunt skills. I can't sing, and maybe you can't play football. But there's one thing we can all do: because of the work Jesus did for us on the cross and through the Resurrection, we can each make our lives count.

We live mission possible because the tough part of the mission has already been accomplished by Jesus. Yes, we have to make hard choices every day. We have to sacrifice. We have to grind out the work. We have to shift and continually reevaluate our priorities. We have to fight sometimes without always knowing the battle plan. We have to learn how to keep fluctuating emotions at bay so our convictions can rise above. And sometimes the days and the moments are just plain hard. We're going to have failures and disappointments, and sometimes we're going to mess up. I know this might sound discouraging, but really it's not.

Make your life count.

Remember the words of Jesus: "In the world you have tribulation, but take courage; I have overcome the world" (John 16:33). I love the Christian Standard Bible translation: "Be courageous! I have conquered the world." When you make the decision to trust in Jesus, you also are a conqueror! (see Romans 8:37).

Life can be so painful at times that it may seem impossible to stay mission possible. But when we maintain an eternal perspective and remind ourselves that Jesus took us from

old to new,
    dead to alive,
        sin to righteousness,
            slave to son or daughter,
                bondage to freedom,
                    darkness to light,
                        lost to found,
we begin to live lives of significance.

In the movie **Gladiator,** Roman general Maximus exhorts his troops with this: "What we do in life echoes in eternity."[2]

Make your life count. This doesn't have much to do with your skill or success or talents. Rather, it has everything to do with the unique calling and purpose God has bestowed on you that He has already equipped you for. It has to do with what He has made mission possible.

Now, let's go live that out!

A SPECIAL INVITATION

IF YOU HAVE JUST FINISHED THIS book and you don't know Jesus in the personal way I've been describing but would like to, keep reading.

Jesus loves you so much that He paid for all the wrong you've ever done. He died on a cross for you and for me, and three days later, He conquered death and rose from the dead. If you believe that, wherever you are, tell Him right now:

Dear Jesus, I believe that You died on the cross and that You rose from the dead. I know that I am a sinner. Please come into my heart and forgive me of my sin. Thank You for forgiving me and trading the old for the new, the darkness for the light. Jesus, I love You and I want to live for You. I give You my life. Thank You for saving me. Thank You for giving me a home in heaven where I will come and live with

You forever one day. Thank You for taking my place and paying my debt. In Jesus's name. Amen.

When you make the decision to trust in Jesus, you are adopted into the family of God. And because God is now your Father in heaven, that makes us brothers or you my sister.

Welcome to the fam!

If you already have made the decision to trust in Jesus and would like to commit to making your life count, why don't you tell Him right now? Say this prayer with me:

Dear Jesus, I believe I can live a mission-possible life because Your mission was accomplished. Give me the courage to do whatever You have called me to do. Remind me that because You have overcome the world, I can do all things that are put before me. Thank You that I get to live mission possible. Amen.

NOTES

Introduction

1. J. R. R. Tolkien, **The Hobbit** (New York: Ballantine Books, 1965), 4.

2. Tim Tebow Foundation, www.timtebow foundation.org/ministries.

3. Mara Gordon, "What's Your Purpose? Finding a Sense of Meaning in Life Is Linked to Health," NPR, May 25, 2019, www.npr.org/sections/ health-shots/2019/05/25/726695968/whats-your -purpose-finding-a-sense-of-meaning-in-life-is -linked-to-health.

4. Reed Tucker, "How Tom Cruise Clung to a Plane in the New 'Mission: Impossible,'" **New York Post,** July 25, 2015, https://nypost.com/2015/07/ 25/how-tom-cruise-clung-to-a-plane-in-the-new -mission-impossible.

5. **Mission: Impossible,** directed by Brian De Palma (Los Angeles: Paramount Pictures, 1996).

Chapter 1: Mission Proposal, Mission Purpose

The chapter epigraph is taken from "Rick Perry: Remarks Announcing Campaign Suspension," American Rhetoric (speech, Columbia International University, North Charleston, South Carolina, January 19, 2012), www.americanrhetoric.com/speeches/rickperrycampaignsuspension.htm.

1. Will Burns, "Research Proves That the Storyteller Is Valued More Than Anyone Else in a Society," **Forbes,** December 7, 2017, www.forbes.com/sites/willburns/2017/12/07/research-proves-that-the-storyteller-is-valued-more-than-anyone-in-a-society/?sh=156c82cc7a15.

2. Lin-Manuel Miranda, quoted in Edward Delman, "How Lin-Manuel Miranda Shapes History," **Atlantic,** September 29, 2015, www.theatlantic.com/entertainment/archive/2015/09/lin-manuel-miranda-hamilton/408019.

3. Lin-Manuel Miranda, "Non-stop," **Hamilton: An American Musical,** Atlantic, 2015.

Chapter 2: God Possible, Purpose Possible

1. Max Anders, **Holman New Testament Commentary,** vol. 8, **Galatians, Ephesians, and Colossians** (Nashville: Broadman, Holman, 1999), 172.

2. **NIV Cultural Backgrounds Study Bible:**

Bringing to Life the Ancient World of Scripture (Grand Rapids, MI: Zondervan, 2016), 2078.

Chapter 3: Right Where You Are

The chapter epigraph is taken from Theodore Roosevelt, **Theodore Roosevelt: An Autobiography** (New York: Scribner, 1922), 337.

1. Martin Luther, quoted in O. E. Feucht, **Everyone a Minister: A Guide to Churchmanship for Laity and Clergy** (St. Louis: Concordia, 1979), 80.
2. "Giving Thanks Can Make You Happier," Harvard Health Publishing, November 22, 2011, https://www.health.harvard.edu/healthbeat/giving-thanks-can-make-you-happier.
3. I understand that there are other Hebrew words for "worship," and I'm not even saying **avad** is the primary Hebrew word for "worship" (because it's not). I'm simply making an observation in how the word has been translated.

Chapter 4: Mission-Possible Superpowers

The chapter epigraph is taken from R. C. Sproul, **In the Presence of God** (Nashville: Thomas Nelson, 2003), 24.

1. Janet Eastman, "Sleep Over Inside the World's Only Surviving Blockbuster Store in Bend," **Oregonian,** August 17, 2020, www.oregonlive

.com/travel/2020/08/sleep-over-inside-the-worlds
-only-surviving-blockbuster-store-in-bend.html.

2. Kevin Hall, **Aspire: Discovering Your Purpose Through the Power of Words** (New York: HarperCollins e-books, 2009), 68, Kindle.

3. **Braveheart,** directed by Mel Gibson (Los Angeles: Paramount Pictures, 1995).

4. Eric Seger, "The Edge: Why Ohio State Chose That as Its Slogan for the 2016 Football Season," Eleven Warriors, August 8, 2016, www.elevenwarriors .com/ohio-state-football/fall-camp-2016/2016/08/ 72779/the-edge-why-ohio-state-chose-that-as-its -slogan-for-the-2016-football-season.

Chapter 5: Purpose in the Present

The chapter epigraph is taken from Vincent van Gogh, "To Theo van Gogh. The Hague, Sunday, 22 October 1882," Van Gogh Museum, 1990, http://vangoghletters.org/vg/letters/ let274/letter.html.

1. Michael Raupp, "What Do Butterflies Do When It Rains?" **Scientific American,** June 19, 2006, www.scientificamerican.com/article/what-do -butterflies-do-wh.

2. Kirshna Ramanujan, "Armor on Butterfly Wings Protects Against Heavy Rain," **Cornell Chronicle,** June 8, 2020, https://news.cornell.edu/stories/ 2020/06/armor-butterfly-wings-protects-against -heavy-rain.

Chapter 6: Purpose in the Resistance

The chapter epigraph is taken from A. W. Tozer, **The Root of Righteousness: Tapping the Bedrock of True Spirituality** (Camp Hill, PA: Christian Publications, 1986), 137.

1. Jordi Quoidbach and Elizabeth W. Dunn, "Give It Up: A Strategy for Combating Hedonic Adaptation," **Social Psychological and Personality Science,** 2013, http://media.wix.com/ugd/c5025f _ba35275363ce8f8886e0f1addcba37d2.pdf.

2. Viktor Frankl, **Man's Search for Meaning** (Boston: Beacon Press, 2006), 113.

3. Alexis de Tocqueville, **Democracy in America** (New York: Literary Classics of the United States, 2004), 617.

4. Dave Ramsey, **The Total Money Makeover: A Proven Plan for Financial Fitness,** Classic Edition (Nashville: Thomas Nelson, 2013), 106.

5. Robert Sanders, "Researchers Find Out Why Some Stress Is Good for You," **Berkeley News,** April 16, 2013, https://news.berkeley.edu/2013/04/16/ researchers-find-out-why-some-stress-is-good-for-you.

Chapter 7: Elevate Convictions over Emotions

The chapter epigraph is taken from C. S. Lewis, **Mere Christianity** (New York: Macmillan, 1960), 117.

1. Helen Keller, **The Story of My Life (with Her Letters)** (New York: Doubleday, 1921), 203.

2. Stuart K. Weber, **Holman New Testament Commentary,** ed. Max Anders, vol. 1, **Matthew** (Nashville: Broadman, Holman, 2000), 169–70.

3. David Jeremiah, "David Jeremiah—Get Your Mind Right," Sermons.Love, https://sermons.love/david-jeremiah/6972-david-jeremiah-believe-get-your-mind-right.html.

4. See Isaiah 6:1–5.

5. See Psalm 11:7; 71:19.

6. See Deuteronomy 32:4.

7. See Daniel 9:9; Luke 6:36; Ephesians 2:4.

8. See 1 John 4:7–16.

9. See Psalm 69:16.

10. See 2 Timothy 2:13.

11. See Exodus 34:6; 2 Kings 13:23.

12. See Isaiah 49:13.

13. See 1 Chronicles 16:34; Mark 10:18.

14. See Proverbs 3:19; Romans 16:27.

Chapter 8: Embrace the Grind

The chapter epigraph is taken from Sir Martin Gilbert, **Winston S. Churchill, vol. 3, The Challenge of War, 1914–1916** (Hillsdale, MI: Hillsdale College Press, 2008).

1. Jeff Davidson, **Common Man, Extraordinary Call: Thriving as the Dad of a Child with**

Special Needs (Grand Rapids, MI: Kregel, 2019), 16, Kindle.
2. Jeff Davidson, "There Is No 'Yet,'" **Goodnight Superman** (blog), July 22, 2016.

Chapter 9: Purpose in the Waiting

The chapter epigraph is taken from Dietrich Bonhoeffer, **Letters and Papers from Prison,** ed. Eberhard Bethge (London: SCM, 2001).

1. Tom Petty and the Heartbreakers, "The Waiting," **Hard Promises,** Backstreet, 1981.

Chapter 10: Your Life Counts

The chapter epigraph is taken from Jim Wooten, "The Conciliator," **New York Times Magazine,** January 29, 1995, www.nytimes.com/1995/01/29/magazine/the-conciliator.html.

1. Rhema Russell, "How I Love Jesus," **Planting Roots** (blog), August 22, 2018, https://plantingroots.net/worship-wednesday-178.
2. **Gladiator,** directed by Ridley Scott (Universal City, CA: Universal Pictures, 2000).

TIM TEBOW is a two-time national champion, Heisman Trophy winner, first-round NFL draft pick, and former professional baseball player. Tebow currently serves as a speaker, is a college football analyst with ESPN and the SEC Network, and is the author of four **New York Times** bestsellers, including **Shaken, This Is the Day,** and the children's book **Bronco and Friends: A Party to Remember.** He is the founder and leader of the Tim Tebow Foundation (TTF), whose mission is to bring faith, hope, and love to those needing a brighter day in their darkest hour of need. Tim is married to Demi-Leigh Tebow (née Nel-Peters), a speaker, influencer, entrepreneur, and Miss Universe 2017. Tim and Demi live in Jacksonville, Florida, with their three dogs, Chunk, Kobe, and Paris.

www.timtebow.com
Facebook, Instagram, Twitter: @timtebow
LinkedIn: www.linkedin.com/in/timtebow15
TikTok: @timtebow_15